Social Sustainability
HANDBOOK
For
Community-Builders

By

Daniel Raphael, Ph.D.

First Edition
Second Printing, 2015

Raphael, Daniel, 1943-
Social Sustainability Handbook for Community-Builders
     ISBN   978-0-692-41640-2
     LCCN: 2015905085

Daniel Raphael Ph.D.
PO Box 2408
Evergreen, Colorado 80437-2408 USA
     daniel.raphaelphd@gmail.com
     303.641.1115

Published in The United States of America.

Font: Book Antigua

Cover Photograph: "Poulsbo Across the Bay" Used with permission.
   Copyright Mary Moff Saurdiff 2015 USA. Facebook: Merry Designs

Author's portrait by Kimberly Anderson Photography

May 17, 2015 ● 09:37

To order this book. or Tee Shirts and Coffee Mugs imprinted with the "Formula For Peace," please visit:

www.socialsustainabilityproject.com

Infinity Press

is an imprint of Daniel Raphael Consulting and Publishing
PO Box 2408
Evergreen, Colorado 80437 USA

Table of Contents

...the security of civilization itself
still rests on the growing willingness
of one generation
to invest in the welfare
of the next and future generations.

Introduction

The emphasis of this book is toward pragmatic applications of social sustainability that can be used by citizens in their local communities to design and implement more sustainable social processes, social policies, organizations and institutions.

"The Basics of Social Sustainability," will provide you with the basic concepts of social sustainability. When you get to the second part of the book, "A Methodology for Community Building," you will be able to understand how those concepts provide insights into designing and building the community you and your neighbors want.

One of the fundamental concepts of this work is that any real, lasting social change that improves the quality of life of ordinary citizens always begins at the local level. Said another way, hierarchies of authority, control and power have almost never been able to develop and complete social programs to improve the conditions of ordinary citizens. All real social progress usually begins at the local level and is initiated by local citizens.

The second fundamental concept is that there always is a vision for what the local community is attempting to do; and this is followed with an intention that guides the work for developing social progress. It usually rests upon that remarkable 1% of every community who sees what needs to be done and then proceeds to develop solutions with their community members and friends. Vision and intention are then followed by a guiding philosophy, mission statement, and the objectives and goals.

The third fundamental concept is that when the vision, intention, philosophy, mission and objectives are validated by the three core values of social sustainability (quality of life, growth and equality) then there is a real probability that your community work will become sustainable in terms of decades and centuries.

The bottom line for any community that chooses to move toward social sustainability is that

> • There must be a fair, uniform and universally applicable method for achieving that goal;

> • There must be a decision-making process that is universally applicable so that anyone can use it to make decisions that support social sustainability locally, nationally or globally;

> • There must be a democratic process of social sustainability that engages the intelligence and wisdom of local citizens for choice-making among sustainable options, and that is easily accessible on a frequent basis.

The fourth fundamental concept involves the conscious intention of guiding the social evolution of local communities using socially sustainable principles and values, compared to the historic and tragic trial-and-error process of achieving progress. This book is particularly devoted to the practices of peaceful social evolution in democratic societies. We have millennia of history that tell us that violence, revolts and revolutions offer a very difficult way of learning by trial and error, to then be repeated over and over again.

While the historic trial-and-error method is evidence of the old paradigm of societies, politics and economics, designing and testing are evidence of the new paradigm of a consciously evolving society that has chosen to move toward social sustainability. Violence and revolution become historic. The process of design and implementation are patently familiar to almost all of us. Those processes can now be used, as they have been for architecture and engineering, to design and implement tested designs to achieve the conscious social evolution of our communities.

Here is a test question for you. In this moment, now, think about what has been said so far. Consider in this moment a simple and straightforward choice of options for the future. Would you choose the old, proven-to-fail paradigm — or conscious social evolution using a thoughtful process of designing, testing, and building peaceful families, communities, societies and nations with transparent intentions? To put this more pointedly, if your community and society were devastated by some calamity of major proportions, would you reinstall the old social, political and economic paradigm, or would you want to create a paradigm that would become sustainable in terms of many centuries?

Without deviation from the norm, Progress is not possible. ~ Frank Zappa

"It is by the decisions of individuals
that our species will be
improved or decline.
It is by the decisions of organizations
that our societies, nations and
civilization will be sustained or die."

The Basics of Social Sustainability

Introduction

Many people talk about "sustainability," but few have discerned the two major areas of sustainability. In this Handbook, we will be discussing social sustainability almost exclusively. To do so intelligently, we must answer two questions, "What is social sustainability?" and, "How does it differ from material sustainability?"

How is social sustainability different from survival, existence and social stability? Is it measureable, and if so, how? What choices are available? And, what do we use to guide our decisions? What makes it important? Why would a society decide to choose to become socially sustainable? What provides the foundation for social sustainability? Lastly, does "trial and error" play any part when a community chooses to explore the development of social sustainability?

While the human species in general understands the fundamentals of material survival and human existence in the short-term, it has not yet learned how to transform itself into sustainable societies. Only a society that is able to question its existence and consciously make decisions to apply the ancient values that have sustained our species for tens of thousands of years will be able to transcend its past.

❖

"There are no shortcuts
for a civilization to
become sustainable.
Only sound intention, moral fortitude
and unflinching perseverance
by citizens
offer the capability of
moving families, communities and whole
societies in that direction."

1
Material and Social Sustainability

Sustainability is a word that has been discussed for several decades, but very few people understand the two sides of sustainability. The illustration below describes this very simply;

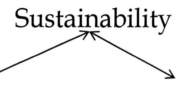

Sustainability

Material Sustainability

**Quantity-Object
Based**

Resources:
Material Environment –
Natural Resources are
valued as material assets.

Sustained by:
Increasing Qty Available;
Decreasing Usage,
Reusing,
Recycling,
Re-purposing.

Social Sustainability

**Quality-Value
Based**

Resources:
Social Environment —
Individuals are valued
as social assets.

Sustained by:
A symbiotic relationship between
individuals and their community.
The community improves the quality of the individual's capability to
participate more effectively in the
community, which increases their
value to their community. Individuals are seen as "social assets"
whose innate capabilities are to be
developed and protected.

Material Sustainability —

- Is quantity-object based.
- The resource for material sustainability is the material environment.
  - → Natural resources: Petroleum, trees, water, air, arable land, mineral resources, etc.
- Material sustainability is improved by: **1)** increasing the quantity available; and **2)** by decreasing usage, reusing, recycling and re-purposing.

Social Sustainability —

- Is quality-value based.
- The resource for social sustainability is the social environment
  - → People – Individuals, families, communities — millions of us!
- Social sustainability is improved by: Improving the quality of people to participate effectively in social sustainability; which increases their value to their family, community and global civilization.

The resource for social sustainability is the social environment — people — individuals, couples, families, communities, millions of us! The way to improve the sustainability of a community is to increase the value of people by improving the quality of their participation in and contribution to their community. A sustainable community assists the individual to develop their inner potential, which almost always allows them to make a meaningful contribution to their community. This is the beginning of a formalized, socially sustainable symbiotic relationship between the individual/family and their community.

Two words are pivotal to social sustainability: quality and value(s). These two words will be used throughout our discussions of social sustainability and when using the Social Sustainability Design Team (SSDT) Process involving the Schematic for Validating Social Sustainability.

Social Sustainability is improved by two efforts: Improving the quality of people to participate effectively in the processes of designing and building a socially sustainable society, and improving the quality of their participation, which increases their value to their family, community and global civilization; and secondly, by a symbiotic response by organizations of that society to assist citizens to do so.

Sustainability, What is It?

Survival. Survival means that our life is in peril now, and all through the day, with the potential of death within this day or the next.

Existence moves our survival into the future, with survival and death still being constant reminders in our daily activities.

Maintenance assures our existence is maintained into an indefinite future. And this is the place where most people and their communities and societies exist — in an indefinite future.

Social stability exists when the stable social, political and economic state of society is balanced. As we are all too aware, now in the early season of 2015, social, political and economic/financial equities are skewed to the point where 1% of the global population possesses at least 50% of the world's wealth and dominates democratic politics. That is a prescription for major social, political, economic and financial upheavals. In a developed democracy, that situation is intolerable simply because rebellion and/or revolt is the death knell of its very existence. Stability in a democracy can only be achieved through the evolution of that nation's political processes.

Social sustainability is the state of social stability that is maintained in social-political-economic balance. Understanding social sustainability begins with the *intention* that brings it into being:

Sustain: To lengthen or extend in duration.
Sustainable: Capable of being sustained.
Sustainability: The ability to sustain.
Social Sustainability: The ability of a society to sustain itself peacefully and indefinitely…, for 5 years, 50 years, 250 years, 500 years and more.

The key to developing sustainable social processes, organizations, institutions and social policies lies in the two words, Quality-Value, (see illustration, page 11) Quality-value is not such an odd concept to accept. We use this every day in the relationships we form. Consider the simple example of two tug-of-war teams. We know that for the tug-of-war to be fair we must have the same quantity-object (number) of members on our team. We also realize that having members with more "quality-value" by being heavier, stronger and better trained in the skills of tug-of-war make all the difference in winning or losing.

Isn't it time we thought of ourselves, individually, in our communities and our democratic processes in the same way? When we do, we will begin to see that equality is a matter of choice to make decisions to increase the social value of people in our societies by improving the qualities of their participation. On a larger scale, social sustainability becomes a matter of conscious choice, not of chance by trial and error.

The world is my country,
all mankind are my brethren
and to do good is my religion.
Thomas Paine 1739-1809

2
Social Sustainability as a Choice

Introduction —

Every community has a small, innovative group of people, usually about 1%, who sees that the principles of social sustainability have something very powerful and good to offer their community. That person will need to ask others in their community if they would be interested in examining the possibilities of their community becoming more socially sustainable and a better place to live. To make that determination, they must sit down and examine the options available to choose from.

Choice-Making with 5 Options —

To create and build a socially sustainable community, a community must first become aware that social sustainability is a choice. This is the beginning of consciously choosing what type of future that community wants. Communities that have come into existence by the trial and error method, as your own, have never survived. If you and your community have determined that you have had enough of experiencing cyclical mistakes, then a conscious decision is needed to begin moving your community toward social sustainability. Doing so will also require a "learning feedback system" to gain the wisdom available from historic mistakes and successes and from your contemporary mistakes and successes.

"Ahhhh," you say, "I didn't know social sustainability was an option! What are my choices?"

1 **"Maintain the Status Quo"** leaves communities to accept their current situation and wait for the inevitable decline of their nation and the social, political and economic implosion of their cities, states, and nation. The key to moving out of that situation is to move out of ignorance of the crisis we are living with. If you are sat-isfied with this "Maintain the Status Quo, that also means being satis-fied with social decline and being satisfied with simply surviving and trying to maintain ongoing existence.

2 **"Fix or Create?"** a) Does your community want to attempt to <u>fix</u> the old paradigm that disappoints you so much; or **b)** do you want to <u>create</u> solutions that bring about social sustainabil-ity in a new social paradigm?

3 **Sustainability for whom?** Is social sustainability just for a special segment of our community? Or, is it something that applies to everyone?

4 **Who and what do you improve to make social sustainability possible?** The best way to improve the possibility of social sustainability is to increase the value of each person in the community by improving the quality of their participation in their community. Because everyone is valued equally, each person should be as well prepared as anyone else to improve the quality of their participation to support everyone's social sustainability.

5 **Is this a top-down decision-making process; or, a bottom-up creative-generative process to move your community toward social sustainability?** Developing socially sustainable com-munities is always a bottom-up, creative-generative decision-making process. National, state, province and district governments can con-tribute to local community efforts by simply supporting those efforts. Just as individuals, families and communities have made the decision to support recycling, they will make decisions in their daily lives to support social sustainability.

Choosing Social Sustainability
Is No Small Decision —

...because there simply are no historic or traditional models to guide that decision. As large as this decision has been described, it fundamentally comes down to a simple "either-or" question: Either we engage the work necessary to move our communities and societies toward social stability and sustainability; OR accept the option of the social decline and extinction of future generations.

...because the very nature of social sustainability requires an "all or nothing" approach to adopting socially sustainable practices. This may seem to be a severe consideration, but because social sustainability involves all of the systems of a society, picking and choosing which social systems to develop to become socially sustainable will jeopardize all of those efforts. Contemporarily, typical communities and societies are composed of social systems that act separately, as though the other systems do not exist. Such half-hearted commitments to social sustainability will not yield half-hearted results, but rather no results.

...because the question of whether to pursue the goal of social sustainability is an all-encompassing question. Social sustainability by its very definition is holistic, requiring everything social to become integrated and connected in a multi-systems relationship. Contemporarily, it is our <u>assumption</u> that they are separate and unaffected by the other things social. It is a dangerous assumption.

...because initiating the conscious social evolution of a community to move toward social sustainability cannot be made by central political authorities. If one sees social sustainability as the only response to the alternative of eventual social extinction, then it becomes an obvious choice for everyone. Those at the top can only facilitate the movement of communities and societies toward social sustainability by consciously staying out of the way as progress is made. The decision must be made by those who will have to live with the consequences of that decision. Only a community founded on democratic principles has the capacity to consciously engage its own evolution, because it requires the conscious effort of every citizen to bring social sustainability into effect.

...because those who make the decision will suffer most from it, as will the second generation. Only those who benefit from that decision, which includes ALL succeeding generations into a sustainable future, will experience with gratitude the sacrifices by those who made such a difficult decision.

...because the decision requires an intentional and fully conscious understanding of the consequences, consequences that are at once both highly beneficial in the long term, but highly uncomfortable in the short term. This involves citizens coming to the realization that the old decision-making morality does not support a socially sustainable society, and in fact actually works against that society becoming functionally sustainable.

...because of its similarities to emigrants who decided to leave their homeland for a foreign frontier of unknown dimensions but of great promises. The first reactions involve culture shock! Making the decision to move a community toward social sustainability offers not just a family but millions of citizens a huge shift in culture. It moves people from the comfortable paternalism of representative democracies to personal responsibility for immediate and personal participation in forming the future they and millions of others must live out. This shift in culture moves finger-pointing from "they" to "us and we," as in "we did this to ourselves, but for the benefit of socially sustainable future generations, for a better society and world."

...because there is no promise of a better life for everyone. Yet everyone in future generations will benefit because the new culture will be based upon the sustainable core values that have sustained our species. Those values are intrinsic to our species and have perpetuated our survival and have made us capable of thriving as a species for over 250,000 years. They are intrinsic to our humanness! But now they must become recognized and expressed in all organizations, social processes and the morality of every community — commonalities that cross all national borders, ethnicity, and political preferences.

...because during the <u>transition</u> from the traditional code of morality to a morality of social sustainability there will occur calamitous debate over the sacrifices that will have to be made. The following are just a few examples of the sacrifices:

- Moving from a "me-ism" culture to an "us" culture;

- Seeing the connection of all social decisions and actions as affecting social sustainability of everyone, not just "myself";

- To give up *assuming* they know the right answers to a conscious awareness of the rightness of every choice-decision-action that supports social sustainability, or not;

- Having to invoke immediate and ongoing decision-making that considers the social sustainability of everyone;

- Holding ourselves personally and morally responsible for the contributions we make toward the social sustainability of everyone, or the appropriations we make for our own selfish sustainability.

- Having the moral courage to hold ourselves and others responsible for the choice-decisions-actions that detract from the social sustainability of everyone.

Systems Thinking. Anyone who is familiar with organizational systems can read between the lines above, "Social sustainability by its very definition is holistic, requiring everything social to become integrated, connected, and in relationship." A sustainable society exists as an integrated system of all the social systems of that society. What our society has been ignoring is that everything in a society is connected to every other social action and process. Failure to understand that fact offers the unconscious probability that a society of unintegrated social agencies is doomed to disintegrate – the ultimate form of "non-integration."

"Peace becomes more and more likely
As societies evolve to become
Socially sustainable."

3

The Timeless Values of
Social Sustainability[1]

Introduction —

As the illustration on page 11 indicates, social sustainability is based on *quality-values:* Quality of life, Growth and Equality. These are the core values of social sustainability that have supported the sustainability of our species for over 250,000 years. They are universal to all people for all time. Our species has persistently striven to *improve its quality of life*, as individuals and as groups of individuals. That persistence is driven by an urge within each of us to *grow* into our innate potential, as we interpret that urge. And, we are driven to explore our potential with the same *equal* necessity as any other person.

Self-evident. The existence of these values is self-evident, though I cannot argue a proof to convince skeptics. Being self-evident these values are held by everyone, though we have ignored them until now. Yes, a developed brain and mind, and an opposable thumb have helped us satisfy our physical needs by being inventive. But they are only supportive faculties to fulfill what urges us onward.

Timeless. These values seem to be innate to our species, which is estimated to be 40,000 to 500,000 years old. Having persisted for so long a time, these values seem to be embedded in our DNA as a "value-set" that is essential for becoming fully human. By their nature, for us personally and collectively, we can consider them to be timeless, enduring and persistent values.

---

[1] The term "value" has a meaning in sociology that is both similar to and yet distinct from the meaning assigned to it in everyday speech. In sociological usage, values are group conceptions of the relative desirability of things. Sometimes 'value' means 'price'. But the sociological concept of value is far broader, where neither of the objects being compared can be assigned a price.

    The idea of deeply held convictions is more illustrative of the sociological concept of value than is the concept of price. In addition, there are four other aspects of the sociological concept of value. They are: (1) values exist at different levels of generality or abstraction; (2) values tend to be hierarchically arranged (3) values are explicit and implicit in varying degrees; and (4) values often are in conflict with one another. Source: www.sociologyguide.com

Universal. Because these three values are typical of every person of our species from the earliest of times and are evident in all people today, we can consider them to be universal to all people of every race, ethnic group, culture and gender. Every person of every race has been equally endowed with these values, to express them as they interpret them for themselves.

Quality of Life —

While life is fundamental to survival and continued existence, it is the <u>quality</u> of life that makes life worth living and gives life meaning. Quality of life is the primary value, with *growth* and *equality* being the subordinate values.

Growth —

Growth is a subordinate value that contributes to the primary value, the quality of life. Growth is essential for improving our quality of life. It is self-evident that growth is essential to our existence and personal and societal fulfillment. To be human is to grow! Having children provides us with a very immediate perspective of growth. As the child grows physically, mentally, emotionally, intellectually, culturally, socially and spiritually they become more human. We did not become who we are without growing. The marks of growth are inherent in children who are full of energy, enthusiasm, curiosity and inquisitiveness! An improving quality of life cannot be attained without growth.

Growth is the natural course of life for individuals, communities and societies. This value ensures that the inherent potential of individuals, communities and societies becomes expressed and fulfilled, which encourages an improving quality of life for everyone. The opportunity for growth promotes the sense of hope, for it is hope that fuels all attempts to progress. And without hope of growth progress is lost; and, can lead to social stagnation and even revolt.

Equality —

Equality is inherent in the value of life. In a democracy, access to the *quality of life* is provided when a person not only has an *equal* right to *life*, but that person also has an *equal* right to *growth* as anyone else. This is what makes immigrants so excited about moving to a democracy — they seek freedom to experience the *quality of life* that makes life worth living — to control their own destiny and to explore their innate potential with the opportunities for growth that a democratic nation provides. We give equal value to each individual, and we would seek to provide more equitable opportunity to every individual to develop their innate potential, as we would our own. Even those with less potential than others have equal value in life to grow by exploring, developing and expressing the potential they do have. Without equality, quality of life is denied to those who could otherwise grow into their innate potential to make major contributions to their own lives and to their community. Then, the community is denied the rightful development of its citizens as social assets.

In a community that has chosen to move toward social sustainability, each person is valued equally because we have come to see the value of each person's potential to make a contribution to the sustainability of every one, all of us. People, individuals, are seen as social assets whose value to their community can be increased by improving their capability to make positive contributions to their own life and others.

Quality of Life, Growth and Equality —

Together, these three values provide an infallible, reliable and universal foundation *for making decisions* among the many options that life offers us individually and for communities. They give support for a sustainable life much as three legs are the minimum requirement for a free standing stool. Life is not socially sustainable with fewer values than these three. This is true whether for an individual, community or whole society. Because of their universal and timeless nature, they are the central organizing, validating and defining requirements *for all organizations* within communities, societies, social institutions, organizations, and the social policies and laws that support social sustainability into the centuries ahead.

Designing sustainable communities begins by writing these values into the founding and organizing documents of organizations. Organizations that have chosen to move toward social sustainability must also frame their vision, intention, philosophy, mission, objectives and goals in terms of these three values. Having done that, they must then ensure that the decision-making processes of their day-to-day activities include those values not as references, but as validators for the accuracy of those decisions and actions.

Generative learning…requires a
conceptual framework of 'structure'
or systemic thinking,
the ability to discover
structural causes of behavior.

Peter Senge, *The Fifth Discipline*

4
The Universal Value-Emotions
That Make Us Human

Quality of life, Growth and Equality
Are not Enough —

Achieving stability and sustainability in a community and in organizations are no assurance that they will also become more humane. If the best of human nature is humane, sensitive enough to be empathic and able to give and receive compassion, then should we not also expect our societies and organizations to reflect the same qualities?

Social Justice and Social Mercy. A family and community will surely become "just" in its moral decision-making simply by invoking the three core values of social sustainability in its decision-making processes. Such a just and lawful society may operate quite well, yet it would not be complete in its efforts to reflect the best of us individually and collectively. In other words, being just would not assure that it would be merciful and humane.

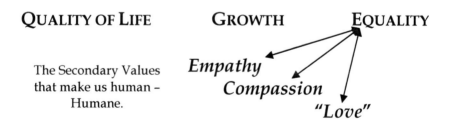

QUALITY OF LIFE   GROWTH   EQUALITY

The Secondary Values that make us human – Humane.

Empathy
Compassion
"Love"

NOTE: I put "love" in quotation marks because love is the summation of its secondary values: Honesty, truthfulness, respect, loyalty, faithfulness, recognition, acceptance, appreciation, validation, discretion, patience, forbearance, forgiveness, authenticity, vulnerability, genuineness, listening, supporting, sharing, consulting, confiding, caring, tenderness and many more. (Source: *Sacred Relationships, A Guide to Authentic Loving,* by Daniel Raphael, 1999)

The Three Core Value-Emotions of
Social Sustainability —

Empathy, compassion and "love" — provide the other half of the innate values that motivate people to act as they do. When these value-emotions are expressed authentically and genuinely, they become the essential connective-energy that empowers our inner potential to blossom throughout the full development of our life from childhood through our elder years. Because we are social creatures, these three value-emotions prompt us to consider others as equals of ourselves, the truest definition of the core value "equality." We see this clearly in the "golden rule," a multi-cultural moral truism; and, we see it in actions of "paying it forward."

Empathy, compassion and "love" are self-sustaining emotions because they allow us to be more open and engaging within our self and with others. They promote the inner development, growth and maturity of our self, leading us to the accumulation of living-wisdom that is essential to guide new generations. Open, confident and socially competent individuals are the essential elements of social leadership, to lead others into actions that sustain families, communities and societies in peace.

What is remarkable about these three value-emotions is that while they are subjective in nature, in reality they can be objectively measured when we observe the secondary values they generate: acceptance, appreciation, recognition, validation, respect, loyalty, faithfulness, trust, authenticity, vulnerability, genuineness, self-identity and identity of others, and many more. These secondary emotional-responses are what make "love" love. They evoke acts of social integration rather than social separation. They are the innate foundations of peace that are so necessary to become fully human as socialized individuals, communities and nations. These value-emotions provide the social lubricant that is essential for the smooth functioning of families, communities and societies, and their sustainability into the future.

A Higher Quality of Life. Fundamentally, empathy, compassion and "love" support the development of a higher *quality of life* for our self and with others. These value-emotions provide us with the motivating energy to *grow* into a more complete, mature and functional individual within our self and within our social environment. They allow us to see the common good as societal rather than selfishly personal. Their expression demonstrates that all others are as valuable (equal) as we are and allow us to express the highest ennobling qualities of human nature at its best — to give example to others that encourages their intra- and inter-personal growth. With these self-sustaining value-emotions, we have the direction and motivation from which to develop highly positive family dynamics before the arrival of children; and a loving, compassionate and empathic means to validate holistic growth in individuals, families and communities.

When you see evidence of these positive emotions in action, you are seeing evidence of the development of self-sustaining families and communities. The positive interpretations of these value-emotions of social sustainability then become constructive to the *social and emotional* sustainability of individuals, families, communities and societies. When we internalize these values and emotions, we realize that the collective power of individuals affects individuals everywhere, as much as the individual affects the collective whole.

People are Innately Good. Just as the three core values of social sustainability are innate to our being, the three core value-emotions are innate as well. Neither set of values are learned behaviors. People, all people, are innately good. The exceptions are those who were raised with predatory values; those who developed negative interpretations of themselves and others; and those who chose to be other than innately good. These three core value-emotions clearly identify us as social individuals rather than as asocial or antisocial beings. These are evidence of being socialized – to care about and for others equally as we do for our self — to be humane.

Defining "Being Human." The six values of social sustainability define the essence of being humane in our relationships with our self and others. They are fundamental to growing into the potential of our self, personality and social relationships. They are innate to our species and exist in us as an impulse to do good. They are proof that people are innately good. We want peace for others as much as we want peace for ourselves because we are wired with the values that make us human – humane.

Peace. The three core values of social sustainability provide the foundation for the three core value-emotions to become society-wide. Peace will only emanate when the innate goodness of others is not only recognized as a potential, but allowed to be developed. Peace is not possible without these three value-emotions being existent and functioning in reality. These value-emotions are fundamental to what we become as individuals, families, communities, societies and nations.

The Raphael Unified Theory of Human Motivation (RUTHM) — You may recall in past *Star Trek* episodes that the Enterprise came in contact with the Borg, life-like beings who were devoid of emotions. Remarkably their society was sustainable, but they had no humanity about them because they could not empathize with others and did not express compassion for others, and were devoid of all traits of "love" as we feel for humanity.

This is a rather stark comparison to what we view as humane – to be human in our best expressions. It points out clearly, as we examine our own being, that we are rational, intelligent beings on the one hand, but on the other we can empathize with others and offer actions of compassion to aid others. Our empathy and compassion comes from our connection to all people, knowing that it could be us as easily as those who are in such a difficult situation. We offer our compassion and aid from our deep inner identification with all others. Without expressing words, we regard ("love") humanity as we are one with others.

This brings us full circle to complete the Raphael Unified Theory of Human Motivation (RUTHM) by engaging the minded-connected side of sustainable social existence and the heart-connected side of sustainable individual existence using the three core values and the three core value-emotions of social sustainability. The following is a real example of that connection.

I have been asked many times, "Why would someone want to initiate a Social Sustainability Design Team in their local community or in an organization or agency?" The question is best answered by someone who actually initiated a Design Team.

First, the person who initiates a Design Team has identified a problem, issue, topic or situation in their community, society or organization that they are concerned about. Second, that person felt an inner urge or need "to do something about it" that identifies their *empathy* for the individuals involved in that situation. Third, that person felt an urge to reach out and offer substantive help (compassion) for those people in that situation. Fourth, that person has a generalized love of humanity, a living connection with those people who are in that situation, which originates from his or her empathetic identification with them in their plight, as this situation could happen to anyone.

The three core value-emotions of compassion, empathy and "love" act in us by urging us to proactively extend our self to come to the aid of others. Doing so, we innately know that their "quality of life" and their potential for "growth" will be awakened in them equally as we know it would in us. This is the innate source for "pay it forward." This is how socially sustainable families, communities and societies begin. It emanates from the very heart of us, and identifies us individually as being humane in our best performance of being human.

RUTHM. These two value systems of our species give us a complete reflection of us as individuals — thinking and compassionate. We are motivated by our intellectual side to devise ways to improve our quality of life, whether that means discovering fire to heat our cave and cook our food or painting water colors as we interpret our world around us. We are also mightily motivated by what we feel from what most call their "heart." We know we are connected to others through our empathy, and we act in compassion to aid those in distress. It appears that all other motivations emanate from these three core values and three core value-emotions, as we interpret them. They reflect fully what we are in the course of being human.

The closest reference to a values oriented theory of human motivation that I could find in an extensive Internet search was *An Overview of the Schwartz Theory of Basic Values,* by Shalom H. Schwartz[2]. Schwartz lists ten values: self-direction, stimulation, hedonism, achievement, power, security, conformity, tradition, benevolence and universalism. There is no dispute with these values, as secondary or tertiary values subordinate to the three core values of social sustainability. They have supported great contributions to the sustainability of our species by many individuals.

The Formula For Peace

$$Peace = \frac{VUCA}{\left[\left(\sqrt[Q\,of]{L}\,GE\right)(EC''L'')\right]}$$

Peace =

Volatile, Uncertain, Complex, Ambiguous

÷

(Quality factored as the square root of Life x Growth x Equality)

X

(Empathy x Compassion x "Love")

> "Love" is measurable by the evidence of its secondary value-emotions: Honesty, truthfulness, respect, loyalty, faithfulness, recognition, acceptance, appreciation, validation, discretion, patience, forbearance, forgiveness, authenticity, vulnerability, genuineness, listening, supporting, sharing, consulting, confiding, caring, tenderness and many more.

---

[2] Schwartz, S. H. (2012). An Overview of the Schwartz Theory of Basic Values. *Online Readings in Psychology and Culture, 2*(1). http://dx.doi.org/10.9707/2307-0919.1116

5
Decision-Making

When we begin using the three core values of social sustainability to interpret all that occurs in our lives and then make decisions based on them, we offer ourselves a timeless and universal means of developing sustainable options, choices, decisions and actions. Those values offer us a consistent and integrated system for taking actions that support and contribute to social sustainability. Those values offer us a method of forming a universally fair code of decision-making that consistently contributes to our social sustainability. Our choices can positively (+) contribute to sustainability, or be neutral (◌), or detrimental (−). Those that are detrimental are "immoral" in terms of social sustainability, whether committed by an individual, or organization or government of any type or size.

What it is. Decision-making that is guided by a set of values is a morality. The three core values of social sustainability, being native to our species, provides us with an "organic morality" that can be applied universally by all people of all nations, races, ethnicity, cultures and genders for all time. Though unrecognized until now, our organic morality has sustained our species for tens of thousands of years. It inherently brings out the good in people, and will continue to guide individual and collective decisions so that our communities become socially sustainable and good places to live in.

What it is not. The morality of the three core values of social sustainability is not a morality based on religion, politics, money, power, fame, race, ethnicity, gender, nationality or personality; and, further, it does not subscribe to those orientations. Because of the nature of these values and morality, it is as applicable to the international community of nations as it is to individuals, families and communities. When used over time to guide the decisions of nations, global social stability and peace become possible. Then our global civilization will be sustained and not perish.

31

Value-Adding Decision-Making —

The six core values of social sustainability are the central arbiters of a socially sustainable moral code for all of humanity. An evolved morality as this accepts and promotes that each individual has an intrinsic and equal value to society. Such an evolved morality demonstrates the necessity of improving the quality of each individual to become a more valuable social asset in their community and society. Such a code of morality adds value to a community as the individual proactively makes decisions that add sustainable value to their own life and to that of their community. Such a code of moral sustainability also proactively adds value to society as organizations make decisions in accordance with these core values.

Quality, value-based thinking and decision-making offer individuals the option of giving organic interpretations to their world. People are valued because they have the capacity to add quality-value to their community and society through their decisions and actions. To increase the value of an individual's contribution to society that individual must be seen as an asset whose value to society can be increased. The individual is an investment, an asset who can develop a "return" to his or her family, community and society. Communities and societies provide services to the individual and family all along the "continuum of human sustainability," (page 107), to improve the capability of their social sustainability. With that in mind, it becomes easier to see how a sustainable morality not only acts to preserve the quality-value of everyone, but proactively provides a more supportive, sustainable social environment.

Teaching Socially Sustainable Decision-Making. By investing in the social sustainability of the family as the primary socializing and enculturation social institution, the child-becoming-adult is prepared to use a sustainable morality. Investing in the social sustainability of individuals, beginning even before conception and continuing through the age of separation from the family, will assure that the family, community and dominant society will become socially sustainable. In this case, society must take on the vision of inventing and creating itself as socially sustainable by adopting socially sustainable practices.

Defining Social Evolution —

A socially sustainable moral code proactively evaluates option
choices, decisions and actions in three ways:

> • + Actions that contribute to the sustainability of another
> individual, family, or community have a positive moral val-
> ue.

> • ◦ Actions that neither contribute nor injure another's ca-
> pability to contribute to the sustainability of their society have
> neutral value.

> • – Actions that detract from the social sustainability of that
> person, another person, family, community, or society have a
> negative moral value.

A socially sustainable moral code provides eminent clarity:

> • To define the proactive behavior of individuals and social
> organizations to promote positive moral behavior that con-
> tributes to the social sustainability of individuals, families,
> and communities.

> • To clearly define immorality — behaviors that
>> **1)** Destroy the potential of (an)other citizen(s) to make
>> a positive contribution to the sustainability of them-
>> selves, their family, community or society;
>>
>> **2)** Diminish the capacity of a person to make a contri-
>> bution to society;
>>
>> **3)** Squander the resources of society as it works to-
>> ward social sustainability; and
>>
>> **4)** Require society to come to the aid of an injured cit-
>> izen to recoup their capacity to make a contribution to
>> the sustainability of themselves, their family, commu-
>> nity, or society; or, support them in their incapacity
>> for their lifetime or until they are healed.

Those who take actions that violate the morality of social sustainability are social predators that create an immense drag on society's forward movement to achieve social stability. I call them "unconscious
social terrorists" who ravage and terrorize their victims not out of

;ious agenda but merely out of their own per-
xample, when an assailant injures a victim, all
sustainability have been violated from a minor
yone who has been a victim's advocate or has
victims of personal crimes will truly appreciate
tic personal injury. It has an effect not only up-
on the immediate victim but also on close friends, family members,
and particularly on a spouse and their children. In some cases the
physical and mental/emotional injuries may endure for the remain-
der of the victim's life; and, all too frequently the injury becomes
transgenerational.

The *Quid pro quo* of Sustainable Moral Duty —

Because individuals are short-lived and societies and civilizations are
long-lived, societies provide the context for the survival of future
generations of individuals, and that can only occur when <u>citizens and
organizations</u> today make decisions that support the survival and
sustainability of those future generations. i.e., "pay it forward."

Most people have forgotten that the *quid pro quo* relationship between
their society and individuals in the past made it possible for them,
today, to have a good life. The social relationship requires that society provide individuals and families with the capability of fulfilling
the three core values of social sustainability. The social *quid pro quo*
relationship of social sustainability also requires that <u>individuals
and organizations</u> make decisions and take actions that support the
three core values of social sustainability for the welfare of future generations; and, they may be required to forfeit their lives to thwart
threats by foreign invaders, or others, in order to aid their society's
survival and the sustainability of future generations.

• This relationship breaks down when the larger society fails to add
value to the sustainability of its citizens, and when it also fails to act
responsibly to curb all influences that are harmful to the social sustainability of its citizens.

• This relationship breaks down when individuals, families and educational institutions fail to teach children how to become

contributing members to the social sustainability of their community, society, and the future of that society.

Socially Sustainable Moral Duty –

The first position of socially sustainable moral duty is neutral – to do no harm to another that impairs their ability to survive, exist and become socially sustainable; and neutral to make contributions to the sustainability of themselves, their family and community. Second, moral duty is proactive to make decisions that contribute to the social sustainability of the individual, their family, community, and to society. The emphasis is on responsibilities that improve the quality of life of the individual, the family and community, and the whole of society, for organizations and individuals. As example, peace contributes to the quality of life at all levels of society. Violating peace violates the social sustainability of all.

1   **The Individual.** Because the individual is at the base of the sustainability of our global civilization, his or her responsibilities and actions are one way: toward self, family, community, state, nation and global community. The individual becomes a value-asset to society as she or he is able to contribute to their own sustainability and to that of their community.

Primary Moral Duty: Preserve life; do no harm directly or indirectly to another.

> **Explanation:** Protect the social and material assets, existent and potential, of social sustainability – the future of that society. Protect and develop those social assets (gene pool, infants in utero, infants and children, and adults) so that added value is given to each person, who has the potential to make a contribution to the sustainable future of society;

Secondary Moral Duty: Make a social contribution to the social sustainability of self, family and community.

> **Explanation:** The first purpose of an individual's life is to make a meaningful life of their own existence; second, to make a meaningful contribution to the sustainability of their

family, community, society, and to civilization. Each individual is responsible to protect, develop and utilize social resources to support social sustainability for this and all future generations.

The emphasis is not only on the survival and existence of themselves and society, but the *sustainability* of that individual *and* society — a society of sustainable individuals in a sustainable social context — enjoying a sustainable quality of life.

EXPLANATION. The illustration, (page 39), explains the *quid pro quo* social symbiosis that develops in communities and societies that have chosen to move toward social sustainability.

2 **Social Organizations — Community and Society.** While "social organizations" includes all organizations even as small as a sole proprietorship, here in this immediate section it is used primarily to discuss civil governments at all levels, companies and corporations, whether at the level of a small village or township to that of state, national or internationally.

The moral duty of civil government in a society that has chosen to move toward social sustainability is to generate its vision, intention, philosophy, mission and objectives that not only aid the survival, existence and operational maintenance of society, but also support the development and evolution of that society into a socially sustainable society. The community and larger society become value-assets to social sustainability when they act to preserve, protect, and develop the social sustainability of its citizens, and remove individuals or associations of individuals who violate the social sustainability of others. Social organizations are as morally responsible to make decisions and take actions as the individual. It is the socially sustainable moral responsibility of organizations to make decisions and take actions that proactively work toward the sustainability of society and individuals.

Primary Duty: Protection and preservation of the integrity of family organization and functions, and then the community of that family.

> **Explanation:** The emphasis is on the survival, existence and sustainability of individuals and families of that society to ensure the sustainability of their society. The individual makes a contribution with their life to that end; and, society aids the individual to have a meaningful, purposeful life that empowers that contribution. It is a relationship of symbiotic sustainability, where the social forces of the individual and society are joined and both benefit without being used by the other for their separate ends. Both have an intention for their mutual benefit.

While this may seem utopian to readers in the early 21st century, it is based on necessary pragmatic moral decisions by each individual and by public agencies that enable social sustainability to develop in a family, community and national society. Individuals accept the sustainable morality of learned behavior that was given to them through the socialization processes of parental and educational instructions — the same as is done today — for the additional purpose of engendering personal guidance for ethical and moral behavior that supports moral social sustainability.

Secondary Duty: To discharge its moral obligations that the public is not morally capable of as individuals.

> **Explanation:** At the level of societal morality, civil government has as its responsibility an obligation to carry out social level moral actions that at the personal level of morality would be considered immoral if carried out by individuals.

3 **Global Organizations — Nations and the Community of Nations.** The moral duty of nations and the community of nations is virtually the same as that of "Social Organizations."

The Three Moral Imperatives
of Social Sustainability —

- No **individual** shall diminish or impede the social sustainability of another person, social entity or global entity without moral justification.

- No **social entity** shall diminish or impede the social sustainability of another social entity, individual or global entity without moral justification.

- No **global entity** shall diminish or impede the social sustainability of another global entity, social entity or individual without moral justification.

"**Social**" relates to more than one individual. "**Entity**" relates to any permanent or temporary social group and may be organized or un-organized. For examples, a corporation, governmental agency and the whole government would be considered permanent, organized social groups. A Tupper Ware® Party and a "Meet Up" cyber group would be considered temporary, unorganized social entities. "**Orga-nized**" relates to a temporary or permanent group that has an organizational structure, even if that means a single organizing person as a sole proprietorship.

An individual has not started living until
he/she can rise above the narrow confines of
his/her individualistic concerns to
the broader concerns of all humanity.

Martin Luther King, Jr.

6
Socially Sustainable Organizations

Introduction —

Societies are not organizations in themselves, but aggregates of organizations and groups of people. Because of that, attempts to move a society to become socially sustainable are not possible, except when the approach strives to urge organizations to evolve towards becoming socially sustainable. This process begins at the local level by designing sustainable organizations *within communities* to provide the foundation for the development of socially sustainable societies. The illustration below shows this supportive relationship very clearly.

Illustration for a Socially Sustainable Society

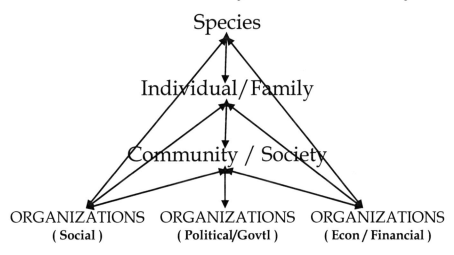

EXPLANATION. The illustration explains the social symbiosis that develops in communities and societies that have chosen to move toward social sustainability. The most powerful organizations are those within the three pillars of a functional society: social, political/governmental and economic/financial.

Priorities of Sustainability —

1. The ultimate priority comes from the genetic mandate to sustain the species.

2. The second priority is to sustain individuals/families to support the continuity of our species. In a society that has chosen to move toward social sustainability, efforts are made to support the social evolution of family dynamics so that families educate and enculturate next generations to become socially sustainable.

3. The third priority is the creation of sustainable organizations. The development of socially sustainable communities and societies is dependent upon the ability of organizations within communities and society to become socially sustainable. Only then will communities be capable to contribute to the social sustainability of individuals and families. Societal sustainability becomes possible when organizations are designed to become sustainable, to stay in business and make contributions to the continuity of society by contributing to the sustainability of individuals and families. This symbiosis is only sustainable when individuals and families also make decisions and take actions that support the social sustainability of their communities, society and organizations.

Contributions by organizations to individuals/families and communities have three symbiotic functions: 1) To aid the sustainability of the species; 2) To aid the sustainability of the individual/family/community; and, 3) To empower individuals, families and communities to be able to reciprocate in that symbiosis by contributing their energies to the sustainability of their mutual society.

A Preliminary Test of Social Sustainability. Existent organizations can conduct a simple test of social sustainability. Using the three core values, they can validate their organization as either contributing to socially sustainability, being neutral, or creating detrimental actions toward the social sustainability of others. 1) Is the intention of your organization to improve the quality of life of our clients, patients, users, etc.? 1a) Do your procedures measurably support the improvement of the quality of life of our clients and others?

2) Do your procedures assist the growth of the inner potential of our clients and others? 3) Do your services and/or products affect each of your clients equally? If you can answer "yes" to each question, it is very likely that your organization is making contributions to social sustainability. A full test would apply each value (quality of life, growth and equality) in greater detail to internal and external policies that would be *validated by measurable criteria of performance.*

Factors that Aid Social Sustainability –

The three core values alone cannot bring about social sustainability. There must also exist conditions that support the efforts of societies to move toward social sustainability.

- **A favorable environment:** Ongoing peace, not war; a stable economy, not depression or hyper-inflation; population maintenance, not over-population; a well educated public, not illiteracy; a responsible system of participatory governance, not despotism, revolution, political apathy or corporate manipulation of democratic processes for their own benefit.

- **Maintenance and regeneration:** A good educational system that allows citizens to develop their innate potential, whether those are great or diminished; A sustaining educational system that transfers cultural wisdom from one generation to another – the wisdom that inherently enculturates the values that support social sustainability. And most importantly, responsible parenting that instills social maturity and personal growth.

- **Functional components:** All social organizations including economic-financial, government, legislative bodies, justice and courts, family practices, education, and corporate policies contribute to the social sustainability of the individual, the family, community, and society. Decision-making at all levels is guided by a complementary three tier morality: individual, social, and global.

The Possibility of Sustainable Organizations —

What is not obvious in the illustration is that in a socially sustainable society, organizations, such as businesses and governments, must learn to simultaneously stay in business and also become major supporting elements in the sustainability of that society. The traditional intention to simply stay in business is naïve. That simple intention must be coupled with the intention to make meaningful contributions that assist communities to not only survive but to thrive and to become sustainable in the process. Doing so, organizations will also thrive.

For social sustainability to succeed, all organizations will need an embedded learning process to recognize that mistakes are learning opportunities to discover what can be learned from them so they do not occur again; and, what supports continued success. This is essential when we consider that almost all organizations were brought into existence without an intention to become sustainable — they are neither "learning organizations" nor adaptable, which are the primary factors of survival, existence, stability and ongoing continuity.

Do not disparage being alone and isolated
on occasion — in 1666 Sir Isaac Newton
avoided the plague when he was holed up
at his aunt's house to invent calculus.
A time apart, a time for reflection can produce
profound insights,
the source of great wisdom.

A Methodology for Community-Building

Introduction

Community-building begins with an individual or group of individuals who want to see that their community grows in ways that lend to its continuance into the future. That is the beginning of an intention for building a sustainable community.

Community-building always begins with a vision and intention. Those two factors are almost inseparable. When the vision comes into one's mind, the intention supports that vision. What is often missing at that point is an awareness of the values that lie beneath to support that vision and intention. Those are almost never revealed right away, and sometimes never revealed in the duration of the community or organization.

Now that we do know the values that support the sustainability of a social enterprise, whether it is a family, local community clinic, educational system, or the community itself, we have a foundation for building the future that lies on the bedrock of social sustainability that has sustained our species for many tens of thousands of years.

What often comes next is for those who initiate community-building to begin thinking of actual buildings, building materials, bank loans, ways to make money for the community, taxes, and so on. In this section, however, we will begin by developing the resources of the community: its community members. Each person comes into life with a mind and the unlimited resources of its potential that can be tapped and used in incredible ways when the right processes are used to engage that potential.

What you will discover in the following pages are the processes that will tap into the resources of the potential of each person who chooses to participate in community-building.

Here are several questions you should consider:

1. Who will come forward on their own initiative to organize a community Social Sustainability Design Team?

2. For what social topic or issue does the team want to begin designing a sustainable solution for?

3. Who is interested in trying out this process for this topic?

4. When and where is your first meeting with these people to discuss the project?

5. What skills do you have that can be used within the team and the role/functions of the team?

6. Do you have 5-11 people who are interested and will begin?

7. Team bonding: This is the glue that will hold your team together, in addition to the curiosity of the team members to see what they come up with for the project. This is a very vital element of the beginning success of the team. Take your time!

Let's begin —

7
Initiating a Community Design Team

Initiating a Community Design Team is very similar to starting any volunteer service group. Whether you are organizing a group of friends to help a neighbor pack up and move to another state, or whether you are organizing to help your community become more sustainable, the process is very much the same.

The Organizer. The role of Organizer is an important one. He or she chooses a topic they hope others in his or her community will become interested in to help resolve the problem. The topic that holds the interest for the Organizer will often serve to captivate and motivate the energy and action of others. Teams usually form around a common interest shared by team members.

Recruiting. Once the Organizer has identified the topic, he or she will begin the process of recruiting team members. The Organizer may initiate recruiting by discovering like-minded people who share the same interest for improving a social issue, social policy or institution in their community. These may be people who are familiar with the Organizer or people with whom the Organizer has a social connection or from their employment. Secondly, the Organizer will also want to recruit people who have skills for the various Team member roles. It should be noted that young people, the unemployed and retired individuals are good candidates because they typically will have more time to devote to such a project. Writing an article in a periodical or other publication might generate interest from those who may be unknown to the Organizer but who share the same interest and concerns.

First Meeting —

Once the Organizer has identified the subject, and recruited a sufficient number of potential members for a design team, he or she will want to invite them to attend a social gathering to discuss matters informally.

The purposes of this informal social gathering include:

> **1.** The Organizer will make the details of his or her intentions known to the group by outlining those intentions and why they are important.

> **2.** The Organizer will discuss the make-up of a design team, the roles and functions within the team and the options for decision-making. Thereafter, potential team members should be invited to ask questions as well as make comments and suggestions.

> **3.** Team building begins immediately. This is a time for the potential design team members to get acquainted with each other and begin the process of bonding as a potential team, and for discovering the "best fit" of each individual in the team.

Some will volunteer and join in, and some may choose not to. Team members who choose to volunteer will want to discuss their qualifications for the various roles of the design team. When enough volunteers for a team (5-11 members) have been enrolled, the role of the Organizer will have been completed.

The role of Organizer is an important role, but it is only temporary. The Organizer usually does not become the Facilitator, but another member of the team often has the skills of a facilitator.

Where do we begin? After getting acquainted and in the early stages of bonding, the team will ask itself, "Now, where do we begin? What do we do now?"

1. The team will need to find *a suitable location* where the team can meet regularly to conduct its business without interruptions.

2. Experience has proven that *the team must meet at least once a week,* in order for the work to progress without interruption and to help team members have a regular weekly schedule they can plan for. Soon the team will discover how necessary it is to plan their efforts and to plan the effective use of its resources — the time and participation of team members.

3. The style of work for the team: Some teams may decide that all team members "do their own thing" and then come back together and discuss those parts. Other teams will work simultaneously with everyone present, and produce in their own way, where everything stays at the same level of progression. Team process is a new way of doing business for most people. You are, in fact, learning how a sustainable design team works. The team and its operation must become sustainable within its operation. It does so by each member keeping their fingers on the pulse and vital signs of team process, so that all elements progress together.

4. Members will soon need to discuss how the team will make decisions. Quorum, majority, 2/3 majority, unanimity, and consensus are available. Although the "flow" of work in the team may become seamless to provide a uniformity of direction when options are exercised, there will come times when an actual vote count will be necessary. It is good to have that worked out ahead of time. To gain insights and wisdom about what is occurring, and the possibility that the Team has blind-sided itself by not exposing a topic that is vital to decision-making, it is time to call upon the Consultant of the team for guidance.

Team Building —

Building a working and functional team involves discovering the common interest that brings people together — for an outcome they cannot achieve by themselves. Each member must provide a willingness to work with others to achieve personal and common outcomes. Working in a design team is as much a process that joins people with their hearts as with their minds. For separate individuals to come and work together, they must first share mutual experiences to appreciate the commonalities of their lives.

Team building is an ongoing and critical element for the smooth functioning of the Design Team. By sharing similar experiences and discovering those commonalities, emotional ties develop – evidence of social and emotional bonding between members that ties them all together in a "shared community" of personal experience. The team building that began at the very first social gathering of potential team members now has become an ongoing facet of the Design Team Process. Team members have begun to see their team as a social process that promotes efficiency, cohesion and creativity that produces outcomes, as well as growth by individual team members.

Feeling socially and emotionally SAFE leads to trust. The Facilitator plays a highly important function almost immediately by facilitating the early stages of team building: The team can only become highly effective when the team has become a framework for positive interaction among team members, where each feels the freedom to express his or her own viewpoints without criticism or rejection, and where each member respects the viewpoint of other team members. Feeling safe emotionally always precedes shared trust and ultimately the confidence in the process itself so that the team achieves focus, unity and direction. Without a firm feeling of being safe, trust will never develop, and the bond within the team will be weak and ineffectual.

A social sustainability design team (SSDT) that has bonded effectively is able to operate without an authority figure, yet possess unity of effort and purpose. Members have roles and functions within the team, yet the process is free-flowing in nature permitting the creative ability of individual members to emerge and contribute to a synergy of effort that far surpasses what individuals working alone can accomplish. An effective Design Team promotes and uses the best attributes, skills and abilities of each member.

This is not an environment where team members can hide their prejudices and biases! Design Teams work best when each member is transparent and humble, and has no agenda, ulterior motives or ego pursuits (power, control and authority). Ego issues and the lack of transparency are contrary to the humility that is crucial to the proper functioning of the team. Though the Team uses the Team Process to expose and identify beliefs and assumptions for their project, the very same process will help team members discover and identify their unsustainable beliefs and assumptions. Uncovering biases and prejudices is not fault-finding.

The result of good team building is a Design Team that is socially sustainable in its own right, thus allowing it to fully develop its full potential. A Design Team must demonstrate within its own operation consistency with the three core values of social sustainability, beliefs, expectations and its own criteria of performance. Members will also discover the value-emotions that make those critical and productive heartfelt connections: empathy, compassion and "love."

A Functional Team Environment. Though the team is not a therapeutic environment, individual agendas and ego manifestations will become very evident in a team environment, and these often work against the productive outcome of the team. This is a nuance of teamwork that must be worked through, and particularly in a team environment which does not use the position of a leader, "boss," manager, director, or *el jefe*. Rather, this is an egalitarian group of individuals who have particular roles that assist the team to function more effectively. When a team begins to work together more than 100 hours, members will find that most of the human problems and human ego/personality disorders become highly evident and manifest, and individual members will either work toward their maturity and growth or opt out of the team. A team will be very fortunate to have a member who is trained in some form of inner personal development, to aid the Facilitator.

As a team member, you are there to assist your fellow team members — not to be a crutch to them, or to enable them — neither are you there to be an antagonist to bedevil them about their shortcomings.

The Consultant's responsibilities include constructively bringing these sticky, personal issues to the forefront of the team. This is different from the Facilitator, who has also become aware of these problems and these resistances, but it is not his/her job to dissolve them — this is the venue of the Consultant.

The Arts of
Inquiry, Discernment & Reflective Thinking -

Inquiry is the primary function of the Design Team: It is the thoughtful business of asking questions, and answering them. The Design Team process is dependent upon the capability of all members to discern subtle aspects and perspectives of a topic that prompts them to ask more questions. When that expires, then it is time for the team to step back from the process, take a break, go aside alone for a few moments and reflect on all that has developed.

It is the duty of all team members to ask questions. No questions, no answers. The best questions are intuitive and cogent to reveal the fundamentals of sustainable social institutions. Students will learn a great deal from Chris Argyris' book, Action Science, which deals with designing organizations that contain an embedded learning component with the capacity to learn from mistakes. The Fifth Discipline, the Art and Science of the Learning Organization, by Peter Senge, discusses organizational systems that lead to learning. It is suggested that you research "inquiry and reflection," "Inquiry and advocacy," and "inquiry process," for guidance on how to ask productive questions.

Reflection. Individual and group reflection is imperative for gaining insights and wisdom about the Team's project. It is a subtle means of accessing inner wisdom. For conundrums, problems or questions that remain problematic and irresolvable even after rigorous discussion, Joseph Jaworski in his book Synchronicity suggests team members should take a recess from discussion, go apart and enter into their own meditative state of contemplation or reflection. By stilling the mind and asking specific questions of the inner Source within them, members will receive the answers and guidance sufficient to move forward.

The beginning of growth for everyone is to take time apart, time aside to reflect on your life and your experiences. Some have seen this as a waste of time as getting nothing done, but it is strongly argued that the most creative moments that have guided the course of our world, materially, spiritually, socially, culturally, psychologically and intellectually in all regards were generated through a time of reflection and contemplation by individuals.

Teams offer a generous opportunity for individual growth, to work in unison with others to accomplish a common goal. The individual grows within themselves and within the team. Yet, there will be times when a team member will need to go aside to consult and reflect within him or herself to consider what is developing. From our personal experiences we must invoke our capacity to reflect, and from reflection we will derive a "lesson" for that individual situation. From lessons, the reflective mind will grasp the over-arching "wisdom" of similar lessons. This is how the individual grows. This is how wisdom is gathered. Only when individuals share their wisdom in team and community settings will societies become great.

Reflective thinking is a very powerful tool. Peter Senge, Chris Argyris and Joseph Jaworski all have much to say about using reflective thinking and reflective action individually and in the team setting as a way of accessing wisdom and insights that are not available during the busyness of life. Reflection involves the relevant experience when we are studying without an agenda, without a procedure for analysis, but rather by the stillness of our mind to do its business more profitably when the conscious side of our mind is still. Unfortunately, few teams will become conscious of the "still water" of movement in the team as a signal to withdraw into stillness and reflection. These reflective moments are when our mind is free to rearrange the bits and pieces we are trying to make sense of. It knows your intention for these moments, so let it do its work.

When team members return to the presence of their team work, then that wisdom and those insights can be shared with everyone. Team members will appreciate that the sum of what members return to the team setting is far, far greater than when they went into their reflective retreats. Minutes of reflection can often reveal far more than hours and days of intense activity striving to do the same work. The secret is "letting" — taking a moment apart from the Team to let your mind take the reins of your inner process to find its direction. Some members may wish to engage qigong, tai chi, yoga or some form of quiet motion as a means of letting the thoughtful side of their brain move into stillness. And, it is very relaxing!

Understanding Design Team Contributions —

In addition to generating designs for sustainable social processes, local Design Teams provide an additional valuable social service to communities, states and nations. By becoming skilled at discerning, weighing, sifting and sorting values and gradients of options, team members evolve into citizens capable of providing mature leadership in their communities, states and nation. Local Teams provide a valuable social service to the sustainability of their larger society by offering the broader public a realistic, validated educational process of how societies become socially sustainable, with citizens becoming more responsible for the leadership of their communities, states and nation.

Because local Design Teams offer their community, states and nation a bottom-up way of developing designs for sustainable social processes, the overall benefits may not be obvious. Hundreds of Design Teams that come together as a system become a perfect setting to bring about positive and constructive social, cultural and political change. Thousands of team members provide a way of "informing" our culture of the realities that are required to underwrite the survival, social stability and social sustainability of our societies. Local Design Teams will be able to examine the fundamental assumptions that underlie their social systems to discern those that are unsustainable, and those that quickly erode like sand when social tragedies wash across communities and nations.

Perhaps the biggest assumption I have made is that people are concerned about their future and that of future generations to become engaged in designing a sustainable future for their children and grandchildren. It is my hope that this is not an assumption but a reality of the character of citizens broadly. But, it takes courage to begin.

Summary —

The design team process and environment involve all the nuances that you have read about—and more. There is an interactive "flow" to the work that is being done that generates synergistic outcomes from the interaction and the insights of team members. Further, lacking a director or an individual who is in charge of the team requires that each individual accept personal responsibility for guiding and leading the team, and to consult with each other on an ongoing basis. Each team member is not separate, yet it is because of their individual uniqueness that each member can make major contributions to the whole integral operation of the team. It is this affective environment that goes on to produce something that is far and above what each member could do individually or consulting by email. This is why it is important that teams meet together as often as they can, rather than apart, so that they can work with this affective environment between and among them.

Yes, the Design Team Process may seem quite nebulous, but team members will experience this flow once they become bonded with each other and begin working together. It begins early in the team-building process so that you become acquainted and get to know each other, to become more effective as a whole working unit. This is not something that can be pointed to on a color chart and say, "This is green 76A," but it is rather a process that you will not appreciate until you experience it. Trust yourself to proceed. Once you have identified and appreciate the feeling of the team process, you will come away from team meetings with an appreciation for each individual and for the work of the whole team. This is an outcome that is not completely measurable in objective, scientific terms.

Strategic planning is worthless —
unless there is a strategic vision.
A strategic vision is a clear image of
what you want to achieve,
which then organizes and instructs
every step toward that goal.

John Naisbitt, *MEGATRENDS*

8
A Framework for Community Building

Introduction —

The prior seven chapters provided us with the wisdom that values and decision-making are the hardware needed to implement any developments we have chosen. Community-building that is to become sustainable into the decades and centuries begins with the values and decision-making that supports social sustainability. Those values are clearly available in the "Schematic for Validating Social Sustainability" (page 119). Local community-building begins at the local level by local community citizens who work in a team setting. Because each team member has a role function to play out while working with the Schematic, everyone can make significant contributions. That value/decision-making process at the local level involves four components that can be easily replicated in almost any Design Team setting.

Four Components of Community Building –

1 **The Three Core Values:**

QUALITY OF LIFE   GROWTH   EQUALITY

2 **The Schematic for Validating Social Sustainability**

The Schematic provides a method for community-building at the local level that supports the sustainability of community organizations, their policies and relationships with their audiences. Validation comes through the transparent process of examining and cross-checking all beliefs (and assumptions), expectations and measurable behavior against each core value in the left hand column of the Schematic.

As a learning device[3], the Schematic offers a workable antidote to the "fragmentation" that David Bohm[4] writes about in his book, On Dialogue. Fragmentation occurs because of the misunderstandings about the beliefs team members hold for any topic. When this happens in the team it provides an opportunity for other team members to ask each person about their differing beliefs. This is the beginning of a process called "Dialogue," as Bohm defines it, which exposes beliefs and assumptions in a gentle and kind approach, rather than arguing their positions.

When differing beliefs are not exposed, misunderstandings occur leading to "fragmentation" in the dialogue. Because fragmentation can occur very easily, the methodology of the Schematic requires team members to diligently examine their beliefs and hidden assumptions when differences arise between team members. The Schematic answers the most pragmatic of all questions, "What works?" to support social stability and social sustainability by examining all beliefs and assumptions using the three core values as the validators of legitimate beliefs that support social sustainability. The Schematic is capable of demonstrating the presence of unproductive beliefs and their underlying assumptions that will eventually undermine social stability and defeat social sustainability.

Using the Schematic and the practices of disciplined dialogue gives members an opportunity to compare and reframe erroneous beliefs and assumptions. This is a vital process of the team: If their assumptions are not exposed but simply included in their designs without validation, then it is very likely the designs will be flawed and eventually fail, leading to the failure of their community-building efforts.

The Schematic and the Social Sustainability Design Team. The Schematic's usefulness is its capacity to develop clarity in

---

[3] Senge, Peter M., *The Fifth Discipline, The Art and Performance of the Learning Organization.*

[4] Bohm, David, *On Dialogue*

fundamental beliefs and their underlying assumptions. It is particularly useful when team members are working on social questions where opinions may run rampant. It ensures that all team members have open transparent beliefs and understanding about what they are talking about and doing.

Because of that capacity, the Schematic is an excellent learning device for identifying and then examining our beliefs and assumptions. It also reveals the matters we neglected to take into account that produce errors, mistakes and inferior performance in failed projects. The methodology of the Schematic allows the Team to develop designs for a social process and social institution that are validated against the three core values of social sustainability. That is, the Schematic is useful for determining ahead of time whether social processes, organizations, institutions and social policies actually have the capability of contributing to socially sustainability. Community-building through "trial and error," although it has been used for thousands of years, is too risky to be used any longer. We now have a means to test and validate the work of social designs before those designs are put into practice. It is a financially sound way to plan and implement social programs, and to measure the effectiveness of grant proposals by philanthropic organizations.

Using the Schematic in a team setting is an ideal place for citizens in local communities to learn about their own beliefs and assumptions and those of their neighbors. As teams multiply, it is expected that socially sustainable beliefs and assumptions will form the foundation for culturally consistent societies regardless of the diversity of ethnic and other subgroups of those societies. Everyone wants to live in a stable society for the long-term — the Schematic and Social Sustainability Design Team Process provide individuals in their local community with the opportunity to do so using a consistent methodology with predictable outcomes.

3 Local Community Design Teams

The Team consists of 5-11 people with 7-9 being optimal. It is not a committee or a discussion group. Members are of equal authority — there is no leader, chief or boss. Team members have specific roles and functions. Each member is also equally responsible for the work of the team.

Teams begin to form when a "burning issue" in the community becomes apparent. Who will initiate the formation of the Team almost always falls on the shoulders of a community volunteer who then discovers others who would like to participate, and then engage in "Team Bonding Exercises" to build trust within the hearts of team members. The Team will need a dedicated time each week, and a dedicated meeting place. Meeting online has NOT proven to be an effective method of teamwork. Too many non-verbal and social cues are missing from interpersonal exchanges, and challenges to hidden assumptions.

Team Roles. These roles develop a synergism as team members begin working through the Schematic.

> **Organizer** – This person represents that unique 1% of every community who sees that something needs to be done in the community and initiates and organizes a local community SS Design Team. The Organizer is rarely the Facilitator.

> **Facilitator** – This person facilitates the work flow and social flow of the team. He/she is NOT a leader or "head of the team," but an equal member of the team.

> **Recorder** – This person does NOT record verbatim, but records the occasional "Ah-ha!" and insight that is shared; and notes the change of topics as the discussion suddenly changes course. This allows the team to pick up the "lost line of inquiry" of the preceding discussion.

Inquiring Members – These members have the pivotal work of asking insightful, connecting questions that open up the topic of discussion. Understanding the "arts of inquiry, discernment and reflective thinking" are essential for the development of topics. Everyone on the team is an inquiring member, and in many ways everyone assists in all role functions.

Consultant – When needed, the Consultant offers the Team a strategic perspective to help the Team see how their project fits into society's progress to move toward social sustainability in terms of 50-500 years.

4 The Design Team Process

The best way to learn about the Design Team Process is to do so experientially, with the whole team learning as it works through the Schematic. The Design Team Process is very similar to the process of developing proofs in a high school geometry class, except several people are working together.

A proof is a written account of the complete thought processes that are used to reach a conclusion. Each step of the process is supported by previously validated postulates, definitions or proofs of social sustainability. In the case where there are no earlier proofs, the team will have to develop those first.

In a Local Community Design Team, team members will fulfill their role-functions by assisting the team to work through the Schematic. Typically, a synergism develops as members exercise their personal skills in their role/functions in the discovery process of working through the Schematic.

The best working teams are those whose members enjoy the dynamics of a team setting, with individuals who have had some experience in the functions of their roles; and whose members are willing to risk not knowing the answers ahead of time; and who have a common interest in the topic that they are exploring. A certain amount of personal humility is necessary to allow the "flow" of the synergism of the Team to surface.

Two Experiential Exercises —

This section is divided into two parts: **a.** This example will teach you how to work with the Schematic; **b.** It provides an experiential exercise. In this exercise you will be in an actual team, in one of the roles of the Team to learn how it functions to help your Team work through the Schematic.

a. **Reading Through an Example.** The methodology of the Schematic is much like using building and construction codes. Building codes can be used to 1) upgrade existing structures to become code compliant, and 2) design new structures according to code. The Schematic can be used similarly: 1) to validate existing social processes, practices, policies and laws, and the design of organizations and institutions as being up to the standard of social sustainability; and 2) to create new, sustainable designs for social practices and institutions, for example. Print several copies of the Schematic, page 121, for your Team.

1. Global Statement of Project: This is the kernel of the sustainable social project you plan to design. For this experiential exercise we will write, **"Reduce Teen Pregnancies, ages 12-19."**

2. Statement of intention. This is directly related to (1.) "Global Statement of Project." According to our example, we write **"Decrease abortions."** Our *project* is to reduce teen pregnancies, and our *intention* is to reduce abortions.

3. AREA OF SUSTAINABILITY: For this exercise, circle **"a. Social"**.

4. State the social project being designed for sustainability. For this exercise, the topic is: **"Child bearing."** Also, write this in the top line as the **"Project"** of the Schematic. It is duplicated here for future reference as you accumulate pages of the Schematic in a file folder, for example. Number the pages consecutively.

5. Venue: Circle: **Individual/family level.** Later, you can scale-up your design to the community level or higher once you have completed and validated the design for the individual/family level. For the sake of this example, it is easier to select the "Individual/family" level because an individual or family is sovereign in how it chooses to manage its own sustainable population.

6. Criteria for fulfillment: (Columns 6 and 7 are directly related to each other.) For every expectation, there are many criteria, behaviors or outcomes that fulfill that expectation. If we expect to reduce teenage pregnancies, then we need to have criteria to measure the progress of the programs we use to make that reduction. *To check the validity of a criterion, measure it against the three core values of sustainability.* For social sustainability to become a part of a community or society there must exist measurable behaviors or outcomes that demonstrate how sustainable expectations are being fulfilled.

Column #6 will become a list of measurable criteria that allows us to assess our progress to fulfill our project (1.). Letter each item as "a", "b", "c" and so on to provide a referencing guide in columns "7. Expectations", "8. Beliefs", and "9. Values." List as many criteria as you can before proceeding. In our example the following is provided:

    a. **Fewer incidents of pregnancies for girls 12-19.**

    b. **Lower school dropout rates. / More graduations.**

    c. **Fewer abortions for this group (reported/projected.)**

    d. **Fewer welfare & WIC enrollments for this group**

    e. **Fewer reported abandoned infants.**

    f. **Fewer infants put up for adoption.**

    g-z. **Add other criteria as necessary to measure your project.**

Provide details for each lettered entry to let the reader know how each criterion will be measured; and, other details as needed.

7. Expectations Column: This column has to do with the program(s) that we <u>expect</u> will fulfill the criteria. In this example we would <u>expect</u> that in order to reduce teen pregnancies, those who become responsible for pregnancies and births to teenagers 12-19 years old would be provided a combination of programs to fulfill the criteria. "Those who become responsible" would include the teenager (boy and girl), his and her parents and community support agencies, for example.

We would expect that...

> • Procreation education programs would have been provided to the parents of the teenager, and long before the teenager becomes sexually active. This prepares parents for socializing, instructing, and enculturating their future teenager with an understanding of the three core values, beliefs, and expectations so the child is prepared to make responsible decisions concerning his or her own sexuality and his or her procreation of a new generation. It is essential that the sexually developed child fully appreciate the consequences of their decision upon the social sustainability of their own life, their own eventual children, and upon the community and society.

> Age-specific and developmentally-specific procreation educational materials are provided to the parents or guardian of the young child who will become a teenager, whether male or female. This would be done early enough in that child's life to answer their natural questions about reproduction, why there are boys and girls, and other topics. These educational materials would relate to specific places in the "Continuum of Social Sustainability," Chapter 12, page 107.

The Expectations Column can be expanded to provide programs as needed for each criterion. For example:

> • Beginning prior to when the child becomes reproductively capable, the child is made aware of human sexuality in ways that are suitable for their age and sexual development. This may include the full spectrum of birth preventative methods from abstinence to sterilization. Those who are capable of reproduction are provided with no-guilt access to birth control devices and medications; and for those who are not yet

capable of reproduction, information about those resources is made known.

As the reader may consider, this technique of information, education, and training can as easily be used for the prevention of tobacco use, drug and alcohol use, anti-social behavior including bullying, peer pressure and many other behaviors that are detrimental to social sustainability. Procreation education in a sustainable society is viewed as any other developmental topic, like acne for example, that inevitably appears in a child's life.

- The thrust of the programs in "Expectations" is to place the responsibility for social sustainability practices upon the individuals who have the most influence to effect a sustainable outcome. At present society is responsible for the support and care of infants-becoming-adults by citizens who had no control of the procreation of that child. That is blatantly unsustainable.

8. Beliefs Column: The lettered items in this column correspond to the lettered items in the Expectations and Criteria columns.

NOTE: <u>Values</u> express as <u>beliefs</u> which spawn <u>expectations</u> that are demonstrated as measurable behavior. When we want to understand how the core values support sustainability, we must consider the expectations that flow from a particular belief.

>>**Core Value:** Quality of life, Growth, Equality
>>**Belief: (& assumptions)**
>> **Expectation**
>>**Measurable Criteria**

Where to begin working the Schematic. The conundrum of where to start to fill out the Schematic, of whether to begin with the Expectations Column, the Beliefs Column or the Criteria of Performance Column is something the Design Team will have to discuss and figure out. For example, you would <u>expect</u> to provide procreation information, education and training only if you <u>believed</u> that doing so would bring about the fulfillment of the Criteria. You must then answer the question, "What leads you to believe that doing so will be effective?" This and similar questions will lead the team to identify the assumptions of those beliefs.

As social sustainability is the final point on the continuum of survival for a civilization, only what supports a society's survival, existence, continued maintenance and sustainability is validated as important. The sustainability of a civilization, nation or society is not dependent upon political positions, for example, but upon what truly affects its sustainable existence.

Our example continued: As we begin to work the Beliefs column, it is time for us to ask about the underlying assumptions we are making about procreation education in a socially sustainable society. ASSUMPTION: That increasing availability of information, education and training to parents-to-be, parents of children, children and reproductively capable young adults will decrease teen pregnancies and decrease abortions. Are there other significant beliefs and assumptions?

- <u>We believe</u> that all sexual beings should become aware of their sexuality as an aspect of their humanness. We believe that this is best provided by the parents or guardians of the child, as a part of growing up. <u>We assume</u> that parents have this information already. Ignorance of the basic functions of human procreation and reproduction contributes to social UN-sustainability for the individual, family, community and global civilization.

- We believe that it is essential that children-becoming-adults are fully informed about their sexuality in order to make mature, responsible, and socially sustainable moral decisions about their reproduction. Increasing awareness must keep pace with their physical development — educational materials that are developmentally specific relating to a child's physical, sexual, emotional and social development.

9. Values Column: Now it is time to cross-check or validate the items in the Beliefs, Expectations and Criteria Columns against the three core values in the Values Column. Validation requires that each of the listed beliefs (and each assumption) is supported by each value and their combination.

10. Statement of Findings. (Page 123.) The Statement of Findings form provides the place to write narrative conclusions that recount the validation by each of the three core values for each belief, assumption, and the criteria that are examined. This is an essential historic record as to whether the Team found the elements supporting the topic as either sustainable or unsustainable. Only Design topics that are validated are used in the final sustainable project.

> **Statement of Findings Example:** Because all humans are sexual by gender, and sexual according to their physical maturity; all people are <u>equally</u> endowed with sexuality, and <u>equally</u> in need of sexual and procreative information, education and training in order to make responsible decisions about whether and when to procreate children. Delaying procreation until the optimum era of an individual's life allows the optimum contribution of <u>growth</u> to their <u>life</u>, and their child's <u>life</u>. Further, it is the responsibility of their society to make available that education as well as birth control devices and medications to reproductively capable individuals; and, it is the responsibility of reproductively sexually capable individuals to avail themselves of those educational materials, birth control devices and medications. These reciprocal responsibilities support the symbiotic social sustainability relationship of the individual, social agencies, and society.

As you can see, the Statement of Findings shows the relationship of the various columns of information in a brief narrative form.

The Schematic allows users to develop socially sustainable ethical and moral social policies for themselves, their own procreative family and their community. Working the Schematic provides a synergistic effect that provides educational awareness and understanding of how social sustainability contributes to the individual's, family's and community's sustainability.

Failure to Validate. Sometimes a social issue is not supported by the three core values. If it is not possible to validate the topic then it is necessary to write a <u>Statement of Invalidation</u> that is also published to avoid duplication by other teams. Teams will find, however, that some aspects of their designs are only partially validated. These need to be published, too.

b. **Working Through an Example.** The following experiential exercise will give you the feel of working in an actual team . It will take 2-6 hours to complete in a workshop situation. Relax, this is an experiential exercise where there are no mistakes — only learning situations. After an hour, your team may feel that "something is just not quite right." If that is the case, stop, examine what is happening and make adjustments.

Please form into Teams with 5-11 people. Do your best to comprise teams with as much diversity with regards to age, race, gender, professional and educational background, etc. [The assumption for having diversity is to bring a very diverse set of beliefs, opinions, and assumptions into the Team for discussion. There is a <u>caveat</u>, however: Great diversity could also become a great impediment to the smooth and rapid development of agreement. Differences between Teams examining the same topic can be discussed later, for everyone's enlightenment.]

Initiating the Team. Although there is no leader of your new team, usually someone will take the initiative to bring several people together into a team. This is good — someone has to initiate the process.

Choosing Team Roles. Briefly discuss the function of each role within the Team and also the training and/or experience each of the members has for the various roles in the Team. With some effort, the team will soon perceive who has capability or even expertise in the roles of Facilitator, Recorder, Consultant and Inquiring Members.

After your first session together, you may want to discuss whether changing roles may be needed.

> **NOTE:** Your immediate work is to select a Recorder even before you choose a Facilitator. This is necessary because almost immediately the Team will begin to experience "lost lines of inquiry" in the discussions. (See "Recorder," page 81).

Facilitator. The person selected for this role will begin to perform his or her duties immediately after selection. You are cautioned to be flexible at the beginning and as non-intrusive as possible. Do not over-facilitate. Just watch, observe, note and in time make facilitative suggestions. Becoming too involved too early will stymie the forward movement of the Team. It is important that each team member be given space for taking responsibility for his or her words and actions.

Inquiring Members. The most active members of the Team are the "Inquiring Members," though every member must ask questions. Their role is to aggressively probe, prod and dig into the topic by directing questions to the group.

Goal. The goal of your Team is to: 1) Fill out the Schematic as completely as possible; and, 2), write a "Validating Statement" if possible.

> **Caveat:** For training purposes, it is not as necessary for the team to complete the project as it is to understand and appreciate the Team Process. This means becoming comfortable with the operation of team roles and the dynamics of interplay of individuals engaged in the team process involving the art of inquiry as you work the Schematic.

Development of Topics for Teams. Because of the limited time of the Workshop, teams should quickly select a topic of general interest. Spend only minimal time determining your topic. If the team gets bogged down, ask the Facilitator to assist in determining your topic. Discuss some topics you would like to work on to validate their social sustainability.

a. This can either be a Vision or Intention; or,

b. The examination of any topic at a stage in the Continuum. Or,

c. Deconstructing an existing social policy, law or existing social organization structure. If the policy is a single statement, it will fit the criteria of a design topic that can be tested in the Schematic. If not, it will need to be divided into smaller parts so that each can be evaluated.[5]

The topic. Every topic will fit into a hierarchy: The global aspects of your sustainability project, a mid-range and the specific topic you will be working on. If your team is unable to reduce the project to a workable size promptly, the team can later reframe the topic as the team progresses. For example, look at the health care system and break it down as follows: sustainable global healthcare system; sustainable community healthcare system; sustainable local clinic; sustainable home healthcare.

Design Creation vs. Implementation. During this creative process of developing designs that you will test for sustainability, do not become concerned with questions, "How will the local sustainable clinic be financed?" Answers to questions such as these and others will need to be raised when your team or someone begins the implementation process of your Team's validated designs. Such considerations may include the population the clinic serves, such as a community clinic for all age groups or that of a clinic on an aircraft carrier, for example.

---

[5] NOTE: "Deconstructing" or testing the validation of a policy can be as simple as examining Human Resource (HR) policies in your company: a) In #1 Global Statement of Project, you would write, for example, "Validate HR Policy #___", and then in "Criteria of Fulfillment" you would write in the specifications of that policy. Next, proceed to "Expectations" where you would want to answer this question, "What expectations would require these criteria?" Then proceed to "Beliefs", and answer this question, "What beliefs would support these expectations and criteria?" And finally under "Values" you would test each belief, expectation, and every criterion against each value, and write a very brief Statement of Findings of your test(s).

Stop the Process. After about 1 hour, Facilitators should bring their Team to a stop and ask the team members how they think the team is doing. Checking with members on the Team Process is a way of "auditing"‡ the unspoken observations of team members.

> ‡ Don't hesitate to ask members if they are using reflective thinking, critical thinking, and "the observer self."

Checking In and Reporting. The workshop facilitator will stop the teams every hour or two to report to the larger group. As this is an experiential training exercise where we learn by doing, everyone's learning becomes more complete in a shorter time by sharing the experiences of each team with the other teams.

Experience and Training. As team members gain experience performing their respective roles within the Team, they begin to realize that each could become immensely more productive and confident with just a bit more training. Team process, team dynamics, team facilitation and many related topics have been meticulously researched by social scientists for the last sixty-plus years. There is a great deal of literature and training available to support the effectiveness of the team you will initiate in your local community.

Techniques for Working the Schematic —

Because the Schematic is flexible in its use, you can begin at almost any place, though all items must be completed eventually for further referencing.

Beliefs. Start with a belief you wish to test for its sustainability and write it in the Beliefs column. Look to the right to the Expectations column. What expectations stem from this belief? Write those down. As you can see, it is not always necessary to fill in all of the blanks of a Schematic to test for the validity of a belief, or expectation. To test the validity of a belief or expectation, you must challenge that belief or expectation to fulfill all of the three core values. If it is not supported by all three values, then it is not validated.

Expectations. This is the other location where you can begin testing. Enter the expectation. Look to the left to the Beliefs column. What beliefs support this expectation? Write those down, and continue.

Validating an Existing Policy or Sustainability Project. Start with a policy, any policy whether it is a family, community, social, corporate, national, international domestic or foreign policy. Or, you could begin with a Sustainability Design feature you wish to test. Is it sustainable and effective? Write this policy or Sustainability Design feature in Column 7, Expectations. Examples may include mandating that health plans provide free contraception to reduce unwanted pregnancies, or restricting visitor access to a state park for habitat recovery. In this case, each Expectation (policy or Sustainability Design feature) must be tied to a particular intention (underlined for each example above).

> **Look Right:**
> **1.** What Criteria would you use to measure whether the policy or Sustainability Design feature works as intended? Write the Criteria for Fulfillment you have identified in Column 6. Using the above example on restricting visitor access to a state park, we might use the population of a recovering and endangered species over time as one of the Criteria for Fulfillment.
>
> **2.** If the policy has been in place for some time, data for the Criteria for Fulfillment may already be available so you can evaluate whether the policy is effective or not. If it is a new or proposed policy, or a feature of a Sustainability Design that will be new to society, then recognize that you will not be able to validate its effectiveness at this point, but will have to wait for it to be tried somewhere for a period of time to measure its effectiveness. It may be validated by the three core values, but its effectiveness may not be apparent, yet.

Look Left:

Beliefs have moral and ethical connotations. They are ideas about how an individual or society should behave that many times are not recognized because they exist in the form of assumptions. When evaluating a policy (or Sustainability Design feature), there are often competing views on its merits and demerits. Each party will have one or more underlying beliefs, whether recognized or not, which motivate them to be in favor of or against that particular policy.

1. Start by identifying the parties in favor of or against the target policy or Sustainability Design feature. In the example above on mandating that religiously affiliated health plans provide free contraception, we might identify religious institutions and the federal government as parties who have competing views on this subject.

2. For each party, try to identify what underlying belief is motivating them to be in favor of or against the target policy. In the above example, religious institutions may be against the policy because they believe that freely available contraception will lead to immoral behavior. The federal government, on the other hand, may believe that individuals must have access to family planning methods to reduce welfare costs. Place each belief in Column 2 along with its respective owner.

Evaluate each belief against the values contained in Column 9. This part requires seasoned judgment to use effectively, and not everyone will agree on the proper conclusion. However, even if no clear-cut answer that everyone agrees upon is achieved, using the Schematic will have served a valuable function in focalizing discussions around the topic of social and material sustainability so that constructive dialogue develops. Additional values to the core values of the Quality of Life, Growth and Equality may be required depending on the situation. These would be secondary or tertiary to the core values, and therefore subordinate to them.

Examining Values, Beliefs and Assumptions —

Please note that dialogue as a process is far different from conversation and discussion. Dialogue in this sense is that unique exchange of thought among several people that seems irresistibly connected, as though without separation, yet allowing the unique contribution each person has to offer. "The discipline of team learning starts with 'dialogue,' the capacity of members of a team to suspend assumptions and enter into a genuine 'thinking together.' " "Team learning is vital because teams, not individuals, are the fundamental learning unit in modern organizations. This [is] where 'the rubber meets the road'; unless teams can learn, the organization cannot learn." (Senge, 1994).

Values form the base of our behaving, speaking, and thinking that we express in our lives and how we live them. They are fundamental to who we are.

Beliefs — To say "values" is to also say "beliefs" because if we value something then we believe those values must be expressed in our lives. And, we further expect those who hold those same values and beliefs also behave as we would. Yet, beliefs and expectations can vary greatly between people who hold the same values. Why?

The reason they diverge so greatly is that while values are universal, beliefs, opinions, and assumptions are cultural, familial and personal. Behavior may vary from one person to the next and from one society to another, even though they hold the same beliefs because of underlying, unexposed assumptions. When you see inexplicable differences such as this, look for unexposed assumptions. Then it becomes time to ask that all important and revealing question, "If we hold the same values, what has caused our beliefs and our expectations for fulfilling those beliefs to be so different?" That is the time for engaging effective dialogue techniques.

Validating Our Beliefs. Caution: Don't get caught up in the "how" question or the "why" question. For example, "How could you, or 'Why did you…? come to that belief from that value?' " will lead you into numerous rabbit holes of speculation. The "why" and "how" questions are not very useful. Rather, it is far more useful to work through each belief by discussing "what" led you to that belief. Examine them without judging them as good or bad, or referring to the individual from whom they came. Further, this can be done easily in a team where you feel safe emotionally and socially to ask questions that will help reveal assumptions. For example, "When did you first begin to hold this belief/opinion/assumption? From whom did you hear this belief/opinion/assumption? And so on.

Within the Team, when differences of beliefs are discovered, it will become necessary for its good working order to examine those beliefs to determine how they contribute to the sustainability of our civilization, national societies, communities, family, and ultimately the individual — not just for this year, but as they contribute to the development of sustainability 50 to 250, and 1,000 years ahead. Yes, 1,000 years is not too much to contemplate. That is why when you think of sustainability, think at two levels, the ideal envisioned future outcome, and the developmental steps that must be implemented to attain that ideal outcome.

Validating Assumptions. Failure to reveal and validate assumptions, either by overt agreement or tacit agreement, will invalidate the results of the Team. Differences of a belief are evidence of assumptions that must be validated separately through the Schematic as supporting or not supporting social sustainability. When differences still persist, it is time to call upon your Consultant for insights and advice. This may seem tedious, but is a preventative procedure that will go a long way to eliminate unforeseen problems and failures of eventual designs. Documenting the validation or invalidation of assumptions will be useful to other teams as they examine similar designs. Differences between the validated results of different teams are indicators that unrevealed assumptions still exist.

We tend to live our lives minute-by-minute and day-by-day with incredible lists of beliefs in mind, never thinking of the unexposed assumptions that support those beliefs. Most of us simply accept the assumptions and expectations that were tacitly attached to those beliefs when they were given to us as children. It is essential for the development of sustainable organizations that their fundamental beliefs and assumptions are exposed and validated.

"Everything is Fine." The development of hundreds of local Design Teams will be able to examine the fundamental assumptions that underlie the social systems of our society. Assumptions are the soft sand that is quickly eroded when tragedies wash across communities and nations. David Bohm tells us,

> "When things are going smoothly there is no way to know that there's any thing wrong — we have already made the assumption that what's going on is independent of thought. When things are represented, and then presented in that way, there is no way for you to see what is happening — it's already excluded. You cannot pay attention to what is outside the representation. There's tremendous pressure not to; it's very hard. The only time you can pay attention to it is when you see there is trouble — when a surprise comes, when there's a contradiction, when things don't quite work.
>
> "However, we don't want to view this process as a 'problem,' because we have no idea how to *solve* it — we can't project a solution." [6]

The biggest assumption that amounts to a grand societal lie is that "Everything is fine." The *Schematic for Validating Social Sustainability* has an uncanny knack for exposing assumptions of team members, their communities, and the assumptions of our culture, larger societies, nationally and internationally. But it takes courage to begin. Perhaps the biggest untested assumption I've made is that the

---

[6] Bohm, David *On Dialogue* (2004): 68.

citizens of democratic nations are concerned about their future, and will become engaged in designing a sustainable future for their grandchildren and their great, great grandchildren. But, then, perhaps they only see that "everything is fine."

Summary —

While most citizens will agree upon the core values, what emanates from them in the form of beliefs seems to always vary in any society depending upon their racial, ethnic, cultural, national, political, religious, and sexual orientations. But, for a community or society to become socially sustainable into an indefinite future, all beliefs and assumptions must be validated by a Values-Beliefs-Expectations-Criteria examination to answer the primary question, "Do these beliefs (policies) work? Do these beliefs and their assumptions contribute to the sustainability of ALL individuals, families, communities and societies?"

Never before has any society, culture, or civilization been challenged with the capability of designing its own sustainable destiny. We have learned only so slowly that when citizens are sustained, their nation is sustained. The work of Jared Diamond in *Guns, Germs and Steel,* and his later book, *Collapse,* points clearly to the necessity of public and organizational policies that intentionally support the social sustainability of citizens, families, communities and their larger society.

Relying upon traditional top-down social and political management and governance practices is no longer sufficient to solve social problems or even delay the inevitable. They are no longer sufficient to lead our people and move our communities and nations into social sustainability. Further, the traditional model of democracy is too slow, too stubbornly invested in established positions, rather than being adaptive and flexible.

Radically new but familiar social processes are needed to consciously create the sustainable future we hope to live in. What is required is an Internet system for training millions of citizens simultaneously via experiential training and educational computer simulation programs for designing sustainable social processes in a Design Team environment. Connecting via public media, citizens would soon see the value of their work as supporting the sustainability of their family and their communities.

Because the three core values of sustainability are universal to all people of all cultures, nations, ethnic groups and racial composition, the synergism of those values and the Schematic can empower local Design Teams anywhere in the world to validate the contribution of their designs. No central authority or control is needed to begin.

> *Caveat* – Patience is required. History demonstrates that it takes many decades and centuries to build a civilization, but only years or decades to decline and even collapse. Building a sustainable global civilization will require conscious and deliberate intention to initiate, and may take decades and centuries to complete — that and an awareness that social change will be a constant annoyance until then.

To enjoy privilege without abuse,
to have liberty without license,
to possess power and
steadfastly refuse to use it
for self-aggrandizement —
these are the marks of high civilization.

9
Social Sustainability Design Team

A Design Team provides a collaborative environment that in some ways represents a micro-image of our society with its beliefs and assumptions, many of which do not support social sustainability. In this collaborative environment, team members are able to explore their roles and develop a synergism as they work with the Schematic for Validating Social Sustainability.

I've been asked, "Why is it necessary to use a team to work the Schematic? Why not use one person who understands it very well to save time?" There are two answers to this question.

First, Design Teams provide a means of accessing the individual and collective intelligence, wisdom and creativity of several people. The creative synergism that develops in a team can produce results that are far more creative and more complete than an individual working alone. Compared to individuals working alone, teams can

- Generate many more ideas and innovation;
- Motivate each other by bouncing ideas off each other;
- Take more risks in their innovation;
- Develop a well-rounded team "personality" that more accurately reflects the social "persona" of society;
- Stay on task more easily – to support the team process both socially and productively for the goals at hand; and
- Create a synergism of personalities, skills, work styles, and team role interaction that is unavailable to individuals, alone.

Second, the team's core purpose is to design sustainable social processes, organizations and policies for example. In order to create sustainable designs that have the potential of lasting 50-500 years, the underlying flaws inherent in the thinking of society that undermine its longevity must be exposed, identified, and tested to determine if they are validated by the three core values. When there is a

1rocedure of dialogue that produces this outcome, the designs of the team will have a far greater assurance of being sustainable in the long term.

The flaws inherent in the thinking of society stem from the beliefs and underlying assumptions that were internalized when the researcher was a child to become unexamined assumptions about everything external to him or her. It is rare that an individual has the skills to isolate and identify the assumptions that underlie the beliefs of his or her thinking. A team of individuals is better able to uncover those assumptions because members are "outside" other member's system of beliefs and assumptions. It requires the inquisitive diligence of a team of individuals to question, test and validate the beliefs and assumptions of each other's suggestions to produce social designs that are sustainable.

Local Design Teams are "learning organizations" as Peter Senge would interpret them. To paraphrase Senge in his book, <u>The Fifth Discipline</u>, "In an era of immense social change, and social and global problems of immense dimensions, no individual has the answer." Design Teams provide a best solution for developing answers that promote bottom-up social sustainability from the collective efforts of everyone in each team, and hundreds of teams across nations.

By operating within the parameters of a Local Design Team, team members learn how to become sustainable as individuals and as a team to influence their communities. This happens as a result of a subtle but significant mind-shift whereby the individual constructs a new mode of thinking. It is this paradigm shift of thinking that transforms not only the individual and team but their communities and eventually their entire culture as these local teams proliferate and begin to transform society incrementally. What we learn from this is that we are not separate. We must shift our thinking from isolation to connectedness and from social fragmentation to wholeness. Finally, we will learn and accept at the core of our being that each of us is inseparable from one another and the whole of everything.

Local teams provide a remarkable hands-on experience for citizens to work with their neighbors, associates and friends to learn how to build sustainable communities and societies. Because most techno-logically developed nations and their economies are knowledge-driven, the team environment will feel comfortable to most people. People enjoy working on a project that they can identify with, where their efforts produce useful results.

Hundreds of local Design Teams represent a new paradigm of social progress that will fill a vacuum of leadership. The products of hun-dreds of local Design Teams will provide a new paradigm of social leadership that reflects the best intelligence and application of wis-dom from society. Bottom-up designs for social action will create a very broad base of intelligent support to overcome the tremendous challenges that await any democratic society in the 21st century. Through the direction found in the efforts of several hundred teams, social leadership is provided without an authority figure.

Roles, Functions and
Qualifications of Team Members —

Though a Design Team is composed of several specific roles, every team member to a degree takes on the functions of every role. The team is composed of Inquiring Team Members, Recorder, Facilitator and Consultant. The preferable number of members is 5-11, with 7-9 being optimum. Too few members inhibits the fluid nature of the team process, and too many limits its effectiveness, making it too flu-id. Too many members often results in distractive side-bar conversa-tions and the potential of cliques.

Inquiring Team Members. The task of asking questions is a respon-sibility of all team members, but it is the primary role of "Inquiring Team Members" to ask diligent, probing questions. Authors Peter Senge, Chris Argyris, and David Bohm all point to the capacity to ask questions as the most meaningful way of exposing assumptions and fallacies while offering the possibilities of acquiring knowledge and wisdom for taking actions that change the outcomes to those that are useful.[7] The team environment provides a socially and emotionally safe venue for members to suspend their assumptions, opinions and judgments. A safe environment is necessary for the team to engage in a free-flowing dialogue among themselves without concern for "stepping on someone's toes."

It is helpful if Inquiring Members have an expertise in the field of inquiry that is without pride or arrogance, and exercise humility when revealing this. Above all they should be curious. It is helpful if they have had some training to develop cogent questions, questions that seem to intuitively lead to unraveling the topics of inquiry.

Because local Sustainability Design Teams are learning organizations that learn about the larger venue of their community and society, team members are also learning about their own personal, inner processes and procedures of inquiry. Teams are composed of individuals who acknowledge the need for reflection and the examination of the procedures of inquiry so that their time becomes more productive. The task of Inquiring Members is vital to what the Team produces, or does not produce. This work is not for dullards and lazy-thinking individuals, but for those who are inquisitive and choose to use their minds and their time effectively.

Inquiring Members should engage one another in a respectful, cooperative and non-judgmental manner. They should respect the different opinions and ideas that others bring to the table even when their own opinions and ideas may differ widely. They should strive to see not as individuals but as team members where the contributions of the group become significantly greater than the value of the sum of the individual contributions alone. It is this synergistic effect of the group process that will achieve the goal.

Inquiring Members should be humble but powerful. They should maintain their focus in the present ("The Now"). They are interested in the work of the team and take notes of their own insights. Doing

---

[7] Senge, Peter M. (1994): 198; Argyris, Chris (1985): 236.; Bohm, David (2004): 70.

so, the team achieves inclusion and integration, oneness, and whole-ness as an element of critical thinking and discernment.

> **NOTE:** Teams will soon realize that their work is tedious, yet as beliefs are validated, there will be no further need to go through the tedious process of a redundant intense examina-tion. There is a "however." However, assumptions that un-derlie each belief will expand as each belief is examined in light of distinct ethnic groups, cultures and nationalities that have their own set of assumptions for that specific belief. As you can imagine, it will be eventual that the clarity of the val-idation of any one belief will become more and more distinct as more and more sub-groups of belief are examined.

Recorder. The Recorder's main function is to record that occasional "ah-ha!" insight, conclusion, or succinct comment that is often forgot-ten. The second function is to observe and note any change in the flow and process of discussion. Often in a highly creative, flowing team process the topic of discussion may change rapidly as members make contributing comments about another topic, leaving the origi-nal topic as a "lost line of inquiry." Having noted that the focus of the team has been deflected, the Recorder can later use their notes to assist the team to refocus on the original topic.

The Recorder takes note of the most important aspects of the team process, and any insights that contribute to the work of the team. Thoughts, insights, conclusions and observations are all valid for re-cording, and later distilled and organized into "findings" or other conclusions of the Team. These may be published separately or with the Team's Statement of Findings (Page 123) or with the Findings of other Teams.

It is not desirable for the Recorder to take verbatim notes, as this would prevent him or her from making their own contributions to the team process. Though deeply connected to the development of answers to questions, the Recorder also takes on the role of "Observ-er." The Recorder's perspective is to pose insightful, cogent ques-tions as well as relevant and reflective answers that are vital to the integration of the validation process. By providing an objective viewpoint, the Recorder provides a valuable contribution to the group process.

Facilitator. There are two functions of the team that the Facilitator is primarily responsible for: one is the social process; and, the other is the production process. It is the Facilitator's function to facilitate and guide these two processes for the most effective development of the Team and its work. It is very helpful if the Facilitator has had training and experience in the areas of team building, team and group dynamics, group facilitation, team processes, and mediation, for example. This role is perhaps the most demanding within the team. The Facilitator must not only monitor him or herself but the team as well, and do so without butting in. The Facilitator provides non-toxic, non-judgmental guidance to team members and working sub-units of the team so the dialogue of the social and work processes advance.

In many ways the Facilitator becomes a trainer of the Team to the extent that training facilitates members in the art of effective inquiry, dialogue, reflection and self-observation. Further, the Facilitator supports members to monitor their own problematic participation, and correct it independently. Often the Facilitator must act as a moderator, or even a mediator, but never an arbitrator.

This person facilitates the group dynamics and team process; monitors the evolution and development of the Team process, and records the conduct, developments, insights, progress and product of the Team; and makes suggestions as to how to improve the Team process. The Facilitator acts essentially as a lubricant, taking action only when necessary to keep the process running smoothly and productively.

Further, the Facilitator should have an awareness of his or her own weaknesses and strengths; and, call upon the Team or outside resources to work with those skill deficits. The Facilitator must monitor him or herself as well as the team in order to avoid being too controlling. Effectively playing this role requires much patience and discernment.

Perhaps the best example of a facilitator is described by John Heider in his book, Tao of Leadership, Leadership Strategies for a New Age. The Facilitator leads by understanding the process of "how" the Team's work is completed, and leads only when the team stumbles in the process. Less is more. Following this method teaches the team how to do for itself as much as possible.

Joellen P. Killion and Lynn A. Simmons, in their book, Zen of Facilitation, 1992, tell us an effective team facilitator:

"• Establishes a sense of community that provides an open, honest and safe environment to share, explore, disagree, and contribute.
• Trusts his/her own intuition...functions from 'gut feelings'.
• Listens carefully.
• Keeps the group on task and moving ahead.
• Stays in the now... rather than diverting to the past or future.
• Reveals the thinking of others in the group.
• Encourages the group to generate their own best solutions.
• Trusts the group's ability to find their own direction.
• Lets go of preconceived notions.
• Models appropriate attitudes and behaviors.
• Develops a "seat of the pants" feel for what is happening and what needs to happen next.
• Honors various perspectives.
• Refrains from only providing his/her point of view.
• Fosters independence...equalizes everyone's sense of power.
• Establishes a sense of safety for group members.
• Regulates group member contributions equitably.
• Assists in bridging one concept or idea to another.
• Guides the interaction through reflective and clarifying questions.
• Moves group thinking from reacting to reflecting.
• Provides nurturing.
• Remembers that he/she is facilitating others' process not his/her own.
• Does nothing when he/she is unsure about what to do."

Facilitating Dialogue. Creating an <u>emotionally and socially safe</u> environment is a crucial function of the Facilitator. A safe environment is necessary for the team to engage in a free-flowing dialogue among themselves and to allow Inquiring Members to ask questions without concern for "stepping on someone's toes."

Typically in the beginning phases of a new Team, the Facilitator will not participate very much in the topics of discussion, but rather monitor the functioning of the Team's processes of dialogue. The Facilitator is there to assist in the development of the Team's discipline of "dialogue," including identifying particular problems that inhibit effective dialogue. Later, as the Team has become more effective and has learned how to monitor and correct ineffective dialogue processes, the Facilitator may become just another participant with little need for ongoing facilitation of the Team.

The work of the team is to come to a convergence of assumptions, opinions, judgments and beliefs about what they are designing. If they are shy to expose their assumptions, it is the Facilitator's job to guide them to examine their resistance. Then he or she will use this situation to train and facilitate dialogue to gain clarity about their resistance, and their assumptions.

Quirky Problems and Stumbling Blocks of the English Language.

> CAVEAT: In this section and the next, "Proprioceptive," may seem complex and unnecessary. It is provided for Teams that have had more experience but are still having problems in the flow of their work. This section may provide some insights into those problems of flow.

As Bohm tells us, "The problems of thought are primarily collective, rather than individual." The following is a brief list of stumbling blocks to dialogue the Facilitator and team will have to overcome:
- The overlay that the English language gives to an English speaking individual's world view;
- Cause-and-effect relationships;
- The linearity of thinking used for problem solution;
- The paradox of "the observer and the observed";

- Shared meaning;
- The pervasiveness of "fragmentation";
- The function of awareness;
- Undirected inquiry;
- and "the problem and the paradox", to name the major impediments to productive dialogue.

Proprioceptive. In all cases, for Bohm and Senge, it is highly important that the members become "proprioceptive," having the ability to be aware of their own thinking. When members practice this technique, they will be able to take the advice of an insightful bumper sticker — *"Don't believe everything you think!"* Becoming proprioceptive is a practiced skill that develops when an individual simply observes what they are thinking, without getting involved in the topics.

David Bohm is particularly instructive in his small book, <u>On Dialogue</u>. [8] To Bohm and Senge, the facilitator's responsibilities include identifying particular problems that inhibit effective dialogue. Bohm identifies dialogue as a process that is far different from conversation and discussion. Dialogue is a process exposing the assumptions and opinions behind the words of the individuals who are engaged in the dialogue. Only by exposing and understanding those assumptions and opinions by the parties involved is it possible to have a dialogue that offers the possibility of clarity and coherence. This is how a society develops internal social homogeneity despite ethnic and other cultural differences.

David Bohm did not anticipate that a device such as the three core values embedded in the Schematic would come into being to facilitate dialogue and validate beliefs and assumptions. The Schematic offers team members a simple device for designing and validating designs for social processes and organizations — and, remarkably, to validate or invalidate the assumptions of those designs the team has exposed, when they examine them in light of the three core values.

---

[8] Bohm, David (2004) *On Dialogue*: 39.

What is vital to the effectiveness of each Team is the exposure of numerous points of view on the same topic, which the Facilitator does with care and compassion. Though those points of view may remain after dialogue, each member has been exposed to those views and the assumptions behind them. *If a community is not operating with the same set of assumptions, and those have not been fully exposed and validated, social problems will surely arise in the future,* if they have not already. In this way we can come to understand why members judge and defend certain points of view. Concerning social sustainability, assumptions, opinions and judgments must be exposed in order to move forward toward the validation of designs the team has developed. As a whole community or nation moves toward becoming integral and whole, Design Teams pave the way toward social continuity and stability. The point of the team's work is to come to a convergence of assumptions, opinion, judgments and beliefs about what they are designing.

Consultant. The Consultant has two main roles to: 1) Provide back-up to the Facilitator. In a rapidly moving team process diversions may occur. If pursued too long they will lead the Team away from its productive course. Sometimes the Facilitator may also get caught up in this diversion. This is much like what happens on the ski slopes when going too fast – getting off track, into loose material, and getting bogged down. And, 2) provide a "centering" function to the Team by maintaining a long-term, strategic perspective to the work of the team. Often the team will become too focused on the immediate dimensions of their work and lose perspective of how their work fits into societal sustainability in the order of 50 to 500 years.

Summary –

The work of the team will be challenging. Its examination of the sustainability of the old, traditional ways of life and morality will put many assumptions and beliefs to a severe test. Our traditional ways of life and morality were never designed for a global society that must accept the strain of moving into a sustainable existence, or succumb to social decline.

I deliberately use the word "moving" because moving toward social sustainability involves the staged implementation of developments. The work of each team is to hold the vision of a sustainable future, and develop reasonable, compassionate, and measurable staged developments for achieving that outcome.

Local Sustainability Design Teams provide an organized and predictable means for developing validated designs for social processes — major and meaningful contributions by local citizens to their immediate communities and to their city, state and national societies. Teams can use the Schematic and their team process for "visioning" sustainable designs for the future. Once the future visioned design is validated, they can begin to develop decremental designs that fill in the blank spaces between that envisioned future and today. Trying to achieve utopian outcomes in one step poses a ludicrous hoax on an uninformed public. Communities and societies now have the tools to consciously evolve socially through a staged evolution to move them toward social sustainability.

"The three core values provide
a timeless and universal
definition of
"the common good"
that brings "social justice" into the
domain of our daily decisions."

In the end, more than they wanted freedom,
they wanted security.
They wanted a comfortable life
and they lost it — security, comfort, and freedom.
When the Athenians wanted not to give to society but society to give to them, when the freedom they wished was
freedom from responsibility,
then Athens ceased to be free.

Edward Gibbon, Historian.

10
Design Team Process

The Design Team Process is the fourth element of the methodology, following the 1) three core values, 2) the Schematic and 3) the Team. The Design Team Process involves the interaction of Team members using their role-functions to work through the Schematic for Validating Social Sustainability. Though the Schematic is inert it provides a familiar procedure for team members that enables the working environment to become highly interactive. A synergism usually develops spontaneously as Team members begin to feel emotionally and socially safe.

The Design Team Process is a highly educational environment also where members learn <u>how</u> to think, rather than <u>what</u> to think. Members who have been trained to work in a Design Team have remarked that their listening skills became sharper while their thinking became more keen and discerning. The best result is that team members learn how to ask cogent, even intuitively incisive questions that lead to clarity in discussions, in or out of the Team.

"Flow" of the Team Process. When the team is in the flow of its work, it is as though time stands still. The flow of the team process takes on a character and "glow" of its own so that the serendipity of insights and participation of the team members occurs when it is needed. There is an underlying awareness among the team members that they "know" the way ahead and their work is on target, useful, and effective.

If available, using a fillable form of the Schematic on a large flat panel wall monitor where the team is working will help keep the members at the same level of accomplishment, and help the team anticipate what is needed to add to or amend the Schematic as new input is developed. As comments are added, other members can modify their own thinking as blank areas of the Schematic are filled in.

It is also valuable to have additions and modifications visible when other members may be working collaterally with support staff or engaged in online research.

The Design Team Process roughly follows the following procedure:
- Fill in the numbered spaces on the Schematic 1-6.
- Identify and record beliefs related to each criterion in #6;
    * Validate each belief with the 3 core values.
★ Expose, identify and record assumptions of those beliefs:
    [Because assumptions are always hidden beliefs in our mind, the only time they become exposed is when someone does not believe what another member may believe. This is a very critical point of the Design Team Process that must not be lost or ignored. At this point, an Inquiring Member must begin a thorough Q and A process with each individual who has differing beliefs to discover "What makes you believe your position is correct?" or words to that effect. Then each assumption must be ...
    * ... validated by each of the 3 core values to the assumption(s) of each individual. Revealing assumptions that are not in agreement with the three core values is essential to the development of sustainable beliefs, expectations and solutions and the removal of unsustainable beliefs, expectations and behaviors.]
    * Recording and publishing the (in)validation of erroneous assumptions is vital to save time for other teams working with similar beliefs and topics, globally. For all Teams to fulfill this function there eventually will need to be a central repository where the association of topics, beliefs and validated and invalidated assumptions must be available to inquiring individuals.
    * Reasonably, once an assumption becomes validated, it also becomes an established and supported belief, and published.
- Write Statements of Findings of what are discovered during the validation process.
- Continue creating a Design based on validations

- Validate the final Design against the 3 core values.
- Write the final Statement of Findings.

Sources of Knowledge and Wisdom —
The sources of knowledge and wisdom used by the Design Team include:

- Using what the members know;
- Investigating historical and contemporary social research;
- Researching archives of wisdom on the Internet and in libraries;
- Entering into moments of reflection where each must reach within and find the Source to guide them toward those ingenious, serendipitous insights that did not exist before.

Mining the Records of History for Its Wisdom —

The wisdom of sustainability is historic and all around us. From historians millennia ago to contemporary historians all have much to say about the reasons societies and civilizations fail. The failures are very pragmatic in what they tell us: <u>Not this way!</u> It is time that we consciously, intentionally, deliberately and conscientiously begin the process of mining the accumulated wisdom related to social sustainability to turn our national societies into learning organizations.
First, we must also create a repository for that wisdom that can be accessed by anyone, anywhere. Second, local Design Teams are an excellent place to begin the mining process because it trains and educates millions of citizens how to become contributors to and collaborators of the future they and their children will fulfill with their lives.

No one in the past has engaged this work with the intention of designing socially sustainable societies. We must be the first to avoid adding our own civilization to the list of failed civilizations.[9] Gathering and writing Statements of Validation must not become just another book of platitudes, but pragmatic wisdom that can be

---

[9] Except, perhaps, *The Lessons of History* by Will and Ariel Durant, 1968, Simon and Schuster. LOC 68-19949.

incorporated into the vision and working policies of sustainable family designs and sustainable communities; and, that those designs become developed into plans, and action taken to invoke their accomplishment.

Consider the following piece of historic wisdom from Cicero, 55 BCE, that alludes to the sustainability of a national economy.
- The Treasury should be refilled,
- public debt should be reduced,
- the arrogance of officialdom should be tempered and controlled, and
- the assistance to foreign lands should be curtailed lest Rome become bankrupt.
- People must again learn to work, instead of living on public assistance."

Example. Economies are a product of human social activity with a very long history. What are the universal, underlying truths, principles and axioms of sustainable economies? We must discover and apply them to stabilize our communities, nation and world; and, avoid the obvious causes of economic destruction. Ironically, we are in possession of thousands of years of experience in hundreds if not thousands of cultures, yet we have not compiled that wisdom to answer the question, "What works economically to support and stabilize our societies?"

Once those principles become known and validated, we must create designs that incorporate them into the training and operation of financial institutions for them to become stable and able to contribute to the economic sustainability of the global economy. History is fairly explicit in its identification of what financial and economic actions do not work, and must be avoided. What we must discover is what does work, and eliminate what does not work. When we generate designs that work through this process, the economy of our societies will become stable.

It seems an obvious development that a small number of design teams with a predisposition for examining historic and contemporary wisdom relating to social sustainability could begin working to discover those universal truths, axioms and principles. Because the three core values — quality of life, growth and equality — provide the validating "truths" of social sustainability, inquiring teams would soon discover the principles and axioms that are universal to the sustainability of all social structures and processes. Hopefully, inquiring teams will begin to "mine" history books and social research sources to collect the bits of wisdom that hundreds of generations of thoughtful historians, writers, thinkers, philosophers and social researchers have shared.

Exploration Tactics by the Team —

There are three primary techniques for using the Schematic. The first involves the process of <u>building</u> a socially sustainable design based on "visioning" some desired intention or outcome, as a social process, organization or policy. Visioning necessitates <u>strategic planning</u> where short-term goals are developed to fulfill long-term goals. Second, you may use the Continuum of Social Sustainability, (Chapter 12, page 107, to guide the development of your social sustainability designs. The third involves testing an existing social process, organization, institution, social policy or law to determine its validity as contributing to social sustainability, or not.

1. Visioning and Strategic Planning are planning techniques that allow us to develop a vision for what we wish to bring into existence through validated designs contributing to social sustainability. Using the Schematic for strategic planning allows us to develop long-range plans and then devise short-range plans that fulfill that vision. Once the future visioned design is validated, then a strategic plan can be developed with incremental short-term goals that eventually complete the strategic plan and vision.

Though visioning offers the potential of developing validated long-term goals, developing short-term goals will be challenging. Planning and implementation must take into account unknown factors that will surely arise that must be addressed. In other words, the plans must be adaptive and flexible with all participants keeping the interests of these socially sustainable plans ahead of any political, financial or social positions that may develop along the way. We must be patient with ourselves to design that future and keep in mind the universal values as criteria for every step along the way.

Start with a larger concept and then divide it into smaller parts. The smallest unit of social sustainability to work with is the individual. You can never go wrong beginning at this level because the foundation of any functional and sustainable society is the individual and the family. If your team begins at the large end of a project using visioning and strategic planning, it will eventually have to work its way back toward the narrow end to validate how that design/vision contributes to the sustainability of the individual.

As example, if you are designing a sustainable local healthcare center, that vision is more palpable and familiar to you than the larger topic of a global or national health care system. You may find it interesting that a socially sustainable local community health clinic has the same rooms, equipment and staff as clinics now, but the intention for its existence and operation is vastly different. You may wish to work with a local clinic as a whole system, and then divide it into its smaller components to be discussed as separate sustainable systems of the clinic. Doing so, you would begin to see how healthcare as a whole is a system that must relate to other social systems, such as education for example.

You would do this before you begin to dissect these smaller parts, and this is what this whole process is about: Taking a larger social system of a global civilization and discovering the subordinate systems that operate within the larger sustainable system. **No social system is sustainable without related and subordinate systems being sustainable, as well.**

This is a process that looks at a great deal of minutia in a very tedious fashion, yet, if you are successful, those designs will not have to be validated again by anyone. If you look at the clinic and then use the Continuum of Social Sustainability to discuss the design of the functions within the clinic, you may find that you achieve more rapid results. You would apply the Continuum to the clinic and discover that one of the earliest functions would be community education, and you would particularly pinpoint that to procreative couples, who were planning 3-6 months beforehand to have a child, or perhaps 2, 3, or 4 years beforehand, and would like to prepare for that time. You would examine the educational services that your clinic would provide, and what staff member of the clinic would provide this, and who is the most skilled. This person may also have the dual function to be the visiting family practitioner, who would visit the family before and after conception and during pregnancy, and who would follow this family unit through the years ahead.

According to the continuum, as the fetus matures and is born, other functions within the local clinic would need to be provided. Rather than having the clinic drive the services, the needs of human beings as physical, social, psychological, intellectual and spiritual beings would drive the design of those services.

You may find a tremendous frustration in your work with this design process if you think of providing service to the current population in your community. In your vision, you may be looking at demographics where one healthcare clinic serves a population of 500 or a 1000 people, with 250 families. As you look at the communities across a large city — such as Green Bay Metro, Wisconsin — you might exclaim, "Oh, my gosh! We need to have 1000 clinics to serve a million people." Thus, you would begin to think in other terms.

Designing a socially sustainable clinic that helps develop socially sustainable individuals may seem to be a narrow-minded approach as you look at the realities around you. While this may seem frustrating, keep in mind that this is only a design to serve the human need to develop a socially sustainable community; and, of course, one of the first places you would start is with healthcare, the multi-levels of healthcare, and then education along the human social sustainability continuum.

Floundering and Finding Your Way Out. If you do not have a design that has some ideals to it, then you will flounder. If you think in terms of only serving the immediate public, then you will also flounder. If you get caught up in "how" to acquire the needed resources — "How do we fund this now?" — and so on, you will flounder.

With a vision, your projection is to not have these particular problems in the forefront of your minds, but rather what services do you need to provide to develop a socially sustainable community for generations to come. Recent literature, for example, cites that some third world countries are providing and developing high-tech solutions to local problems without having to hire experts. There are intelligent people everywhere who go to libraries to figure out how to do what needs to be done with the materials and resources at hand. When you do it this way, then you become very inventive, very creative and you will find that you will then have **local, enduring solutions.**

2. Using the Continuum of Social Sustainability (page 107) focuses the efforts of the team on the individual and his or her needs at any point in the continuum of his or her life by examining their physical, mental, emotional, social, intellectual, cultural and spiritual needs at each stage of an individual's life. Doing so, your team may address the individual's educational and economic needs, as well as their capacity to make contributions to the sustainability of his or her family, community and society. When a team uses this approach, it will necessarily begin with the procreative couple who initiates the beginning of that new person. It follows along the continuum to the point(s) where the Team chooses to examine and design sustainable practices for the individual, either within the family of origin or in a later era of the individual's life.

3. Testing an Existing Social Process, Organization, Institution, Social Policy or Law for Validation. Testing an existing social process, social policy or the structure of an organization involves deconstructing the originating organizational documents, such as charters, constitutions, by-laws or policies and analyzing their parts from the standpoint of validating their sustainability. For example, if you evaluate a legal statute or law, you would first look to the expectations associated with it. List these in the Expectations column of the Schematic. If the statute or law provides a sanction for violation or a reward for compliance, list these in the Criterion for Fulfillment column. When you find assumptions, and you will, list them in the Beliefs column to validate them later when the team is working on the column.

Next, the Team would proceed to discover the fundamental beliefs that underlie the operation of the organization that support the Expectations and Criteria provided in the policy, law or regulation. Some organizations state their beliefs in the early part of these documents, which are usually associated with its philosophy and intention for its existence. List these in the Beliefs column.

The last process involves the validation of the social sustainability of those underlying beliefs, expectations, and the desired performance that measurably fulfill those expectations. If the policy, law or regulation does not support <u>quality of life</u>, <u>growth</u> and <u>equality</u> of the individual, family, other social organization/institution, or society, then it is not validated to support social sustainability. When a policy, law or regulation, etc., is unable to be validated as supporting the three core values of social sustainability, then it must be revised, replaced by one that does, or removed.

Conclusions –

Social Sustainability Design Teams may be far off the chart of reality for most people in the 21st century, but consider the following:

- The problems we now face are global. Yet, our civilization has developed without a plan for sustaining itself.

- Numerous global, civilization-threatening problems have developed that endanger our civilization's continued existence: food and water shortages, decreasing arable land, overpopulation, natural resource limitations, economic instability, militarism and political instability, and increasingly destructive natural cataclysms, to name only a very few.

● Futurists, scientists and historians agree that earth's civilization, as it exists and as it grows larger, is unsustainable. The decline in the number of people and the quality of life is inevitable, and, it appears, imminent.

● These problems are so complex, so pervasive and so huge in scope as to be insolvable by any one government/nation or combination of nations even if those problems were identified and the solutions were obvious. Political position-taking, power-authority-control conflicts, resource acquisition and allocation conflicts between political parties, nations, and large corporations, and public malaise will prevent timely action to alleviate the problems.

● The necessity of developing socially sustainable solutions at the community level becomes rather obvious when we consider, 1) No person has ever had the experience of a planetary manager to administer a planet; and, 2) No one living today has the capacity to bring the resources that are obviously available to heal the problems described above. The only resource that is readily available that has the talent, breadth of service and sheer numbers needed to begin healing the unstable and unsustainable nature of our global culture are the people who have the most to lose and the most to gain — millions of citizens in thousands of local communities.

Without innovative solutions from the bottom-up at the local community level to move our societies toward social sustainability, our civilization is likely to go the way of many dozens of civilizations that have risen, peaked, declined, and disappeared, (Diamond, Jared). Implementing design solutions for social sustainability must emanate from the people who will enjoy the benefits of their preparedness, or suffer from their lack.

11

Validating Policies and Laws; and the Socially Sustainable Morality of Pending Court Cases

In Chapter 10, *The Design Team Process,* we discussed the process by which the Design Team could design social policies, the design and structures of organizations and even the intentions of social institutions to support the evolution of a community to move toward social stability and social sustainability. Once designed or validated, those designs and intentions then are already in moral compliance with the moral values of social sustainability; and, when applied by organizations and individuals in their decision-making processes those decisions, too, will comply with that morality.

The six core values of social sustainability are more than a code of ethics. They are a code of morality because decisions based on those values have a life and death effect in the end upon the survival of individuals, families, communities and the whole of human civilizations. In this chapter I will strive to show how that code can be used to validate existing policies and laws and to test the socially sustainable morality of pending sensitive court cases.

In Chapter 10 we were striving to design and create new, socially sustainable policies. In this chapter we will be striving to validate existing social policies and laws and pending sensitive court cases as supporting those values, or not. We will be using the same example that began on page 60, but we will be examining those issues from the moral perspective, using the Schematic for Socially Sustainable Moral Validation, page 121.

An Experiential Exercise — Part 1

Using the Schematic for Socially Sustainable Moral Validation for Testing Existing Policies, Designs, Processes, Legislative Bills, Statutes and Legal Cases.

~ Schematic for Socially Sustainable Moral Validation ~

Moral Question or Issue: <u>Is Amendment 1 of the United States of America Constitution,</u> ["Congress shall make no law respecting the establishment of religion, or prohibiting the free exercise thereof; or abridgement of the freedom of speech, or of the press; ...."], <u>in moral compliance with the 6 core values of social sustainability</u>?

1. Global Statement of the Project: "Does social sustainability support the publication and provision of education and training materials concerning human procreation to individuals age 20 and below to reduce teen pregnancies, ages 12-19?"

2. Statement of intention: This is directly related to "1. Moral Question." According to our example, we write **"Reduce Teen Pregnancies"**. The moral issue is the publication of relevant material to reduce teen pregnancies, and our *intention* is to reduce pregnancies in this group.

3. Area of Sustainability: For this exercise, circle **"a. Social"**.

4. State the moral issue being validated for social sustainability. For this exercise, the issue is: **"Free Press, Child Bearing."**

5. Venue: Circle: **Individual/family level;** Circle **State/Region,** and Circle **National.** These three are circled because each has an investment of sovereignty involved in the moral question.

At this point the top section of the form has been completed.

An Experiential Exercise — Part 2
Developing Social Programs
to Fulfill the Moral Question

This exercise will complete the bottom half of the Schematic for Moral Validation by developing example programs to "Reduce Teen Pregnancies / Reduce Abortions." The Moral Question is a response to the development of these Social Programs.

> **NOTE:** <u>Values</u> express as <u>beliefs</u> which spawn <u>expectations</u> that are demonstrated as measurable behavior. When we want to understand how the core values support sustainability, we must necessarily consider the expectations that flow from a particular belief.

> **>>Core Value:** Growth (Quality of Life, Equality)
> **>>Belief: (& assumptions)**
> **>> Expectation**
> **>>Measurable Criteria**

Items 6 – 9 for this example are virtually identical to the text provided on pages 61-66. There are, however, perspectives for those Items that must be considered, and which are provided here.

6. CRITERIA FOR FULFILLMENT: These are the desired measurable outcomes that would become known when the programs listed in the **EXPECTATIONS** column are provided.

7. EXPECTATIONS: This column provides a clear perspective of the operational Symbiotic Relationship between citizens and their society:
> * The Expectations column contains the programs that we EX-PECT will fulfill the Criteria of Performance listed in Column 6. Symbiotically, the programs are provided by society, which would fulfill society's half of that relationship. The other half of that symbiotic relationship would be provided by the parents of the child-becoming-adult, and by the child who would participate in those programs.

* Because socially sustainable programs are initiated at the local community level in a bottom-up process, *do not expect* that those programs would be administered by a governmental agency.

* The moral challenge stems from the programs. Objections by opposing sides will be initiated due to differing beliefs and un-examined assumptions of those beliefs.

8. BELIEFS/Assumptions Column: Simply list all social beliefs about the topic your team is considering that you believe support the moral justification of publishing educational and training materials for indi-viduals related to population management.

A. We believe, in accord with the morality of social sustainabil-ity, that withholding the facts of procreation prevents the opti-mum arrival of new citizens. ...that children brought into the world before the parents are prepared to raise their child or children to become sustainable individuals is immoral. With-holding the facts of procreation to procreatively capable indi-viduals is immoral‡ — a violation of the social sustainability of the community, society, and the global civilization.

B. We believe that it is immoral to withhold this information and training because it violates the symbiotic relationship be-tween the individual/family and society to support social sus-tainability.

‡ "Immoral" is defined in context as any behavior that prevents, diminishes or removes the social sustainabil-ity potential of an individual/family, community or other social organization, society, and the global civili-zation, as determined by the three core values.

C. If it is our *belief* that procreation should morally contribute to the social sustainability of individuals, families, communi-ties and ultimately the global civilization.

9. VALUES. The three core values of social sustainability (quality of life, growth and equality) are values by which all beliefs, expectations and criteria of behavior are validated as sustaining the development of socially sustainable individuals/families, communities and societies. The validity of these values lies in their existence in our species for over 250,000 years and that they are universal to all people of all nations, societies, cultures, races, ethnicity and genders. They are the final arbiters of sustainability for our species in all regards.

Statement of Findings for the Individual/Family —

The Statement of Findings provides a more detailed, narrative, discussion of how the three core values were used to design social programs and to validate moral issues. Here is a continuation of the above example applied to the Statement of Findings form.

The moral question: "Does the morality of social sustainability support the provision of education and training concerning human procreation to individuals age 20 and below to reduce teen pregnancies, ages 12-19?"

> **Quality of life:** The quality of life is more fully assured when informed, conscious and intentional procreation takes place at the optimum point in the life of the prospective mother, father and child. **YES.**
>
> Explanation: Premature pregnancies deprive the mother, father and child the opportunity of a higher quality of life to grow into the full potential of their social, emotional, physical, intellectual and spiritual maturity equally to others who consciously plan conception and pregnancy.
>
> **Growth:** The growth and maturation of the individual, (mother, father and child), is more fully assured when informed, conscious, and intentional procreation takes place at the optimum point in the life of the prospective mother, father, and child. **YES.**
>
> Explanation: Premature pregnancies prevent the optimal course of maturation and growth that support the social sustainability of the mother, father, child, family, community and society.

Equality: The value of each member of the potential procreation is equal when procreation occurs when it is preceded by informed, conscious and intentional decision-making at the optimum point in the life of the prospective mother, father, and child. **YES.**

Explanation: Premature pregnancies deprive the mother, father and child the opportunities of a more mature life to access the benefits of life equally as others who have waited to initiate conception. Their value to the community and society to aid their own sustainability and that of their own family, community, and society is diminished by the responsibilities of premature parenthood.

The moral question: " Is Amendment 1 of the United States of America Constitution, ["Congress shall make no law respecting the establishment of religion, or prohibiting the free exercise thereof; or abridgement of the freedom of speech, or of the press; ...."], in moral compliance with the 6 core values of social sustainability?

Yes. Explanation: The above Statement of Findings for the Individual/Family demonstrates the consistency of this Amendment and the six core values of social sustainability. "

Validating the Moral Sustainability of
Legislative Options and Pending Court Cases

Legislative Pass/Fail Test. For any community or society to become socially sustainable into an indefinite future, all beliefs must succumb to the scrutiny of the Schematic for Validating Social Sustainability and the Schematic for Socially Sustainable Moral Validation to answer the primary question, "Do these beliefs (policies) work? i.e., do these beliefs contribute to the moral social sustainability of all families, communities and societies?" To examine the socially sustainable moral contribution of a law or public policy, we would ask, "Does this statute or public policy contribute to or diminish the social sustainability of individuals, family, community, society, and civilization?"

Pending Court Cases. The values of social sustainability are already paraphrased in the Declaration of Independence, and in the Constitution and Amendments. That is sufficient in itself to explicitly use the core values of social sustainability (quality of life, growth and equality) that have sustained our species for over 250,000 years to argue those cases more objectively in light of those values. The expansion of political and civil rights has become complete over the duration of the United States' existence. Yet, social rights have not yet been explored and developed to the same extent. Now they can be.

Arguing court cases using only political and civil rights without including the holism of social existence does not fully appreciate the necessity that courts also take on the duty of protecting the social rights and social sustainability of this and all future generations. This gives the courts a wide, new role in the proactive work necessary to develop the social sustainability of future individuals, families, communities and societies. Court cases have always used precedent as a means to extending the interpretation of political and civil rights. That is historic in nature.

Applying the self-evident values that have sustained our species for so many tens of thousands of years provides the courts with long established precedents of those years to adjudicate cases so that their findings extend that precedent of social sustainability into the future. In those findings, the court can simultaneously adjudicate current cases, and potential cases for all future generations.

Implementing the Work of Design Teams —

Because the three core values of sustainability are universal to all people of all cultures, ethnic groups, racial composition and nationalities the synergism of the three core values can empower local "Sustainability Validation Teams" anywhere in the world to validate the social sustainable morality for social questions and the operation of organizations, institutions, public policies and statutes.

Teams by their very operation will provide a learning environment where individuals and families will become more fully aware of

the effect of sustainable social values upon their larger society to become morally responsible for their actions. The effects of social sustainability will become personal and societal.

Because of the universality of the values, sharing results between
teams, globally, will empower constructive change of older systems
of social institutions and policies in all cultures and nations to become more universally and morally socially sustainable. Developing
moral designs of social sustainability is truly an ideal that requires
progressive stages of designing and planning the programs that lead
to sustainability. Once the plans are formed an *implementation team*
must devise developmental steps for implementing those plans that
lead to greater and greater social stability with consideration for
them also being morally socially sustainable.

❖

"A democratic society will only become sustainable
when the combined decisions and actions of
individuals and organizations
work for the same goals of sustainability.
Both have an equal influence upon
the survival and sustainability of
future generations.
Both are required to maintain the continuity of society
by preventing social disintegration
and ensuring that society evolves evenly.
Only then will society provide an improving quality
of life and the potential of
equal growth for everyone."

12
The Continuum of Social Sustainability

The continuum of social sustainability for the life of an individual describes an ongoing series of influences that begins months before conception and continues until his or her death. The continuum describes a course of life where numerous physical, mental, emotional, social, intellectual, cultural and spiritual influences can be brought to bear upon the individual to best prepare him or her to support their own social sustainability, the procreative family he or she may develop, and the social sustainability of their community and society. Several questions for the individual and society need to be answered to address the symbiotic relationship between the individual and their community and society, "How then does the individual contribute to their own sustainability? How does society contribute to the sustainability of the individual? And, "How does the individual contribute to the social sustainability of their larger society during their lifetime?"

Significant Eras in the Continuum include, but are not limited to the era before conception; pregnancy; the first year and subsequent eras of growth and development, until personal independence from the parental family. These are arbitrary eras that must be adapted to the developmental stages of the child/individual. Independent adulthood continues until the individual chooses a mate, or chooses not to; and, to eventually become a parent, or not to. Later stages may include the eras of career(s), family; mid-life; post-family; early elder years; elder years, and death. These broad, loosely defined eras are provided only to give the reader a general understanding of the developmental continuum of individual social sustainability.

Each era of the continuum provides the individual, their community and society with opportunities to prepare the individual to successfully engage each later era. Children, teens and young adults are provided with the knowledge, skills, and training to procreate and raise their own child(ren) to become socially sustainable individuals. The training, education, and all preparations provided to the individual to enhance their own social sustainability would be for nothing if those preparations did not also support the social sustainability of the family, community, the larger society and ultimately their global civilization.

An Imaginative Illustration. While it is well nigh impossible to graphically illustrate the process of designing sustainable social institutions to satisfy the evolving hierarchy of needs of an individual through the continuum from pre-conception through his or her elder years and on to death, the reader will find below a brief and narrow narrative description that may be of some assistance.

Imagine the course of life of an individual as a vertical line on a chart that is approximately 9 feet tall that begins at the bottom of the chart before conception and continues to the top at death. Numerous eras of development can be charted for the individual on this long, vertical continuum of life so that the vertical line eventually comes to look like a tree trunk with many branches of influence from individuals and social agencies attached to the trunk.

At the bottom **1)** are two vertical lines representing the father and mother. At **2)**, the horizontal dashed line represents conception and the beginning of the era of pregnancy.

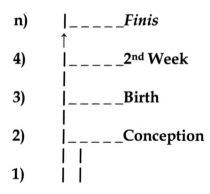

Briefly —

CAVEAT: **The following description is for a society that has chosen to move toward social sustainability.**

In each era preparations are made for engaging the next and following eras with training, education, information, and skill development to enhance social sustainability of the individual as he or she engages the next era.

1) Pre-Conception.

- Both parents-to-be have been determined not to carry defective genes that would lead to genetic anomalies of their children; and are certified for procreation.

- The procreative couple has begun diets specifically designed to provide for the healthiest sperm and ovum for their child.

- Both have received training and education for establishing a stable social, economic, emotional, and domestic environment (for example) before conception, after conception, and during pregnancy.

2) Pregnancy.

- This stage is all about preparation for birth and the first year.

- This includes diet and nutrition for the mother,

- Education for the parents-to-be concerning the emotional-social environment of the mother-with-child, and father;

- Home visits by a local health care professional with expertise and loving support and mentoring for this era;

- Education concerning the first year that is formative for the psycho-spiritual-mental-emotional health of the child and the requirements of co-parenting. (And more.)

3) Birth – 2nd Weeks.

- This is the brief era where trust develops. Feeling safe is the foundation for building trust at any age, but is essential at this age as it forms the underpinning for all personal and social trust. As the child consistently feels safe, secure, nourished and nurtured the development of trust in this early era forms the foundation that gives rise to all other positive emotional developments in weeks, months and years to come.

4) 2nd Weeks – 1st Year.

● More education and training is provided to develop healthy diets and eating habits; visits by the healthcare professional; preparation for parents-as-models; the beginning of social training, continued development of trust, and more.

n) ...all the eras in the continuum until death.

Every developmental stage in the individual's continuum provides numerous opportunities to support his or her physical, emotional, mental, social, intellectual, cultural and spiritual development. Within each stage the individual is given access to the resources of social institutions to aid his or her potential for becoming a sustainable individual. These are the "branches" of influence on the vertical axis of the continuum where social institutions contribute to the developing and evolving sustainability of the individual.

In a capsule, the most important developmental eras of the individual's life occur between pregnancy and through age twenty, approximately. A partial list would include education, training, physical supports, and the social and emotional supports that help bring the individual into becoming a "socially sustainable individual." This achievement usually occurs in his or her 20s or 30s after they have left home and when they are prepared to choose to become a procreative partner, or not. The contributions of social institutions continue throughout the individual's life, until death; and in return the individual continues to make decisions and take actions that contribute to the social sustainability of their family, community and society. In this way, the symbiotic nature of the relationship between individual and institution is strengthened and maintained.

As this process continues through each stage of the individual's development, and as the individual becomes more capable of becoming sustainable, social institutions need to become more capable of contributing to the individual's social sustainability. These two developments are what build a sustainable community, society and civilization. To that end, design teams must begin to examine social institutions for their capacity to contribute to the sustainability of society; and, to design them to make that contribution to individuals, families and communities.

Sustainable Social Institutions —

Because the three irreducible core values have sustained our species for over 250,000 years, these values lend themselves to validate the designs for social sustainability to give all societies the potential of becoming sustainable for centuries.

Three levels of social sustainability designs: Individual, social, and global. When we begin to think about the needs of individuals, even before they are born, we begin to <u>anticipate</u> their arrival and <u>anticipate</u> their needs at various levels of their capability; and, then we begin to <u>anticipate</u> the needs of their families, our communities and our societies. When you think of this continuum model, think not only of the individual, but think of the continuum of human social sustainability for organizations that serve the social continuum of the life of the individual. All the efforts to develop responsible, socially sustainable individuals will never come to fruition until there are concurrent efforts to develop social processes, agencies, organizations and institutions with validated socially sustainable designs. For those "branches of influence" to be effective and of lasting influence on the individual, organizations of all types must become socially sustainable.

Social Systems. For a whole society to become socially sustainable, all social institutions that support the social existence of individuals, families, communities and society must become an integrated system of systems, where each social system participates in an integrated system of all other organizations and institutions. When you examine the spectrum of social institutions, even within one nation, it becomes very evident that the evolutionary development of our global society is very primitive — particularly when it is compared to what would be desirably consistent with the three core values of social sustainability.

As you can surmise, social institutions[10] will have to undergo a progressive evolution to transform themselves into sustainable organizations consistent with the three core values. The old competitive philosophies of "profit-above-all-else" and "winner takes all" of doing business will change. It will change because the old models and world image of businesses do not contribute to the social sustainability of a rapidly evolving social world. In order for business to survive it must reinvent itself to not only sustain itself, but to proactively aid the sustainability of our communities, families and individuals.

While the design work of teams may seem idealistic, team members will come to see their projects as practical applications of the three core values in the designs they are striving to implement. It is not beyond comprehension to envision that other teams may simultaneously deal with the strategic planning of long-term and short-term implementation in developmental stages to support those designs.

If we take education as an example, we in the early 21st century would ask, "What would the intentions of a socially sustainable education system look like?" (The Illustration on page 39.) The answers are many, but very consistent according to the three core values of social sustainability:

- Education that contributes to the sustainability of our species' survival, existence, and sustainability;

- Education that contributes to the sustainability of the individual/family who contribute to the sustainability of our species, their communities and societies;

---

[10] http://plato.stanford.edu/entries/social-institutions/

- Education that contributes to the evolution of organizations to contribute to the social sustainability of the individual/family and communities;

- Education that contributes to the *quality of life* of the individual;

- Education that contributes to the *growth* of the individual by encouraging him or her to explore and develop their inherent potential;

- Education that is provided *equally* to each individual, according to their inherent capabilities.

- A socially sustainable educational system would provide the necessary education and training to the procreative couple, pregnant couple, new parents; and, to the child when he/she is capable of exploring their potential.

- A socially sustainable educational system provides developmental stage assessments for the individual along their life's course.

- A socially sustainable educational system provides placement recommendations commensurate to the individual's assessed capability, rather than arbitrarily by age.

- A socially sustainable educational system does not perpetuate competitiveness between parental couples, their children, or between other individuals. The only competitive venue is within the individual to better their own performance, as satisfaction in their own achievements.

- A socially sustainable educational system educates and prepares individuals to thoroughly understand and to know how to socialize and enculturate their own children, or potential children, in the moral, ethical, and social requirements for living in a socially sustainable family and community.

- A socially sustainable educational system would teach the child from the earliest ages throughout the lifetime of the individual in the fundamentals of social living that supports individual and societal social sustainability.

- A sustainable education program enculturates and pre-pares the child to frame their existence within this symbiosis so that they are prepared to aid the sustainability of future generations with responsible behavior today.

Because the human mind has an infinite capacity to learn and grow, education is a perennial feature of a sustainable society that begins with the parents before the birth of their child, and continues through childhood and through the continuum of his or her lifetime.

If we take healthcare as another example, we would have to ask, "What would the intentions of a sustainable healthcare system look like?" The answers are many, but very consistent according to the three core values of social sustainability:

- Healthcare that contributes to the sustainability of our species' survival, existence, and sustainability;

- Healthcare that contributes to the sustainability of the in-dividual/family who contribute to the sustainability of our species, their communities and societies;

- Healthcare that contributes to the evolution of organiza-tions within the system of healthcare to contribute to the so-cial sustainability of the individual/family and communities;

- Healthcare that contributes to the *quality of life* of the indi-vidual. It is not sufficient to support a bland quantity of life, but that continuation must also maintain the quality of the patient's life, which includes the seven spheres of every per-son: physical, mental, intellectual, emotional, social, cultural and spiritual.

- Healthcare that contributes to the *growth* of the individual by encouraging him or her to explore and develop their in-herent potential in all seven spheres.

- Healthcare that is provided *equally* to each individual, ac-cording to their inherent capabilities.

- A healthcare system would provide the necessary educa-tion and training to the procreative couple, pregnant couple, new parents that supports their social sustainability; and, to their child when he/she is able to begin exploring their sexual potential.

• A sustainable healthcare system provides developmental stage assessments for the individual along their life's course, for example.

• A sustainable healthcare system is primary for a society to maximize its potential to become sustainable — not just to maintain physical health, but proactively to generate the good (sustainable) health of society. Healthcare and education of-tentimes operate together to reinforce their messages and in-fluence upon the individual throughout the entirety of an in-dividual's life.

In many ways a socially sustainable healthcare system looks very similar to a socially sustainable educational system, and is as holistic. It begins to influence the quality of life of the individual even before birth. It continues through all of the developmental stages with the intention of assisting the individual to develop and live a sustainable quality of life. It includes sub-sections such as nutrition and diet, spiritual-emotional-mental-intellectual-social health, physical devel-opment and maintenance, for example. It, too, has an ongoing as-sessment program that engages at each developmental stage of the individual and its own system's capability to do so. A sustainable healthcare system has as its primary intention to develop, improve and/or maintain not only life, but the quality of life as well. The ob-vious eventual and inherent conflicts between maintaining life and maintaining the quality of life for a patient will need to be examined in the context of a morality that contributes proactively to the social sustainability of society.

The Symbiosis of Service —

As the social sustainability of individuals is continuously enhanced through the influence of parents, social agencies and institutions, they are continuously instructed and encultured to make decisions and take action that support the social sustainability of their family, community and society. The individual and social agencies make decisions and take actions that support social sustainability for their mutual benefit. The interplay and relationship between the individual and society is very symbiotic throughout the entirety of their life.

The most fundamental symbiotic decision by the individual is to delay procreation until he or she is mature enough to raise their own children to become socially sustainable; and, to limit the number of children they do procreate to two or three — enough to replace the parents. Societies have dual responsibilities, obligations, in this symbiotic relationship: First to protect their citizens from social predation by decreasing its incidence; and, secondly to socialize, educate, and indoctrinate the child-becoming-procreatively-capable in the responsibilities of procreation in a socially sustainable society and civilization.

When this relationship is out of balance, the population of that society will proliferate past the limits of material sustainability, which then endangers the social sustainability of the society, leading to societal decline and collapse. There is considerable evidence of this in our own contemporary global situation. This imbalance is made worse when there exists a pernicious culture of selfish individualism — "It's all about me!" In our contemporary culture there are no socially sustainable moral requirements for individuals to make socially responsible decisions and actions that contribute to the social sustainability of themselves or their community, society, or the larger global civilization. The results, as we are seeing, are moral degradation, social disintegration and general social decline.

When the relationship between the individual and their community and larger society is out of balance, then societies proceed toward collapse, as we are seeing all too clearly in the United States and other developed nations in this early part of the 21st century. When individuals do not make decisions and actions that support their society, then we see the beginning of the end of a society and community that will eventually become unsustainable, collapse and disintegrate.

What we are not seeing today is even a modicum of socially responsible decisions by individuals toward society, or of the social agencies toward the social sustainability of individuals and families. The symbiosis that is needed must become a conscious and intentional part of child rearing from the child's earliest years through their young adulthood until they separate from their family of origin. Society truly needs moral leaders to point out the symbiotic responsibilities of communities, cities, states and nations to enculturate and instruct their citizens in their mutual responsibilities to create and then maintain socially sustainable communities and their larger society.

Success may generate courage and
promote confidence,
but wisdom only comes from
the experiences of adjustment to
the results
of one's failures.

"The responsibilities of social sustainability
are not silly expressions of
philosophic idealism,
but opportunities that
assure future generations
will continue our traditions of
an improving quality of life,
with even greater opportunities to
grow into their potential,
and that of their society.
Faithful fulfillment of our responsibilities to
our children's great grandchildren
will assure that there will be a
better society,
better democracy
and better economy for them
than we enjoy today."

~ Schematic for Validating Social Sustainability ~ Project: _____ p. ____

1. Global Statement of Project: _____

2. STATEMENT OF INTENTION (briefly): _____

3. AREA OF SUSTAINABILITY: a. <u>Social</u>   or   b. <u>Material</u> ?   (Circle one)

4. State the social project being designed for sustainability (e.g., family, childrearing, community, education, health care, economy, commerce and trade, governance, or other) :
   OR
   State the material project being designed for sustainability:

   VENUE: → Individual/Family   →Community   →State/Region   →National   →Global Region   →Global

- -

6. CRITERIA FOR FULFILLMENT (See #1)
   (This should be measurable)
   We observe

7. EXPECTATIONS
   *We expect....

8. BELIEFS
   (and assumptions)
   *We believe....

9. VALUES
   *We value....

*Quality
Of Life

*Growth

*Equality

"Progressive social evolution
will not be possible until
leaders and the people
realize that the hope of
a better nation –
and a better world –
is bound up in the progress and
enlightenment of the individual."

p. _____

~ Schematic for Socially Sustainable Moral Validation ~

Moral Question or Issue: _____

1. Global Statement of Project: _____

2. Statement of Intention (briefly): _____

3. Area of Sustainability: a. **Social**   or   b. **Material ?**   (Circle one)

4. State the social field of the moral issue being validated e.g., family, childrearing, community, education, health care, economy, commerce and trade, governance, or other) : _____
   OR
   State the material project being morally validated for social sustainability: _____

5. VENUE: → Individual/Family   →Community   →State/Region   →National   →Global Region   →Global

   -

6. CRITERIA FOR FULFILLMENT (See #1)
   (This should be measurable)
   We observe

7. EXPECTATIONS

   *We expect.....

8. BELIEFS
   (and assumptions)
   *We believe.....

9. VALUES

   *We value.....

Quality
Of Life

Growth

Equality

"There are no shortcuts
for a civilization to
become sustainable.
Only sound intention, moral fortitude
and unflinching perseverance
by citizens offer the capability of
moving families,
communities and whole societies
in that direction."

~ Statement of Findings ~ Project: _____

Contact Persons: _____

eMail: _____

Telephone: _____

Date: _____

p. _____

The Project is   VALIDATED   INVALIDATED   (Circle one)

Statement _____

_____

_____

_____

_____

_____

_____

_____

_____

_____

_____

_____

"We could predict then,
as Peter Senge suggests,
that when we change
the structure of democracy,
that change will cause a change in
behavior of citizens and leaders.
We could go further
and even predict that
citizens and leaders will begin to *think*
in terms of the integrated systems
of democracy and social sustainability,
and *behave* accordingly."

Acknowledgments

The acknowledgment of all those who have given me advice, counsel and guidance and even expert knowledge over the last 40 years is far too numerous to recount. For everyone who has given me encouragement or expert knowledge, "Thank you!"

Giving thanks to my dear wife, Sherille, is grossly inadequate to say with words. Few know the sacrifices that a partner makes for a disciplined and persevering writer and author. She does! Thank you, Lovey.

To one particular person who has guided my literary efforts for the last 14 years, but who wishes to remain anonymous, my "Thank you, Mate!" seems vastly inadequate to convey my appreciation for his support and tenacious encouragement. He has been responsible for many book design and book cover decisions.

To Marthe Muller in South Africa and my dear friend Hilarie Anderson of Indian Hills, Colorado — Thank you for reading through the book. Your comments have given me great encouragement to proceed ahead, knowing that readers will have much to reflect upon and enjoy.

I would be grossly out of place were I not to thank Providence for arranging my life such that I have had the flexibility to read broadly, think, contemplate, meditate, take notes and write, revise and write some more. The willingness to live a humble life also goes a long ways to live a life where meditation, writing, thinking and contemplation come first.

"To move this nation and the
democratic global culture into
the 2nd paradigm of democracy,
leaders in all organizations
must be taught and trained
how to reframe their thinking from
political processes
that support democracy to
social systems
that support sustainable democracies."

Bibliography

Argyris, Chris., & Schön, D. 1996
   Organizational Learning II,
   Addison Wesley, Reading, Mass.

Argyris, Chris, Robert Putnam, Diana McClain Smith 1985
   ***Action Science, Concepts, Methods, and Skills for Research
   and Intervention***
   Jossey-Bass Publishers, San Francisco

Bohm, David 2004
   On Dialogue, Ed. by Lee Nichol, Preface by Peter M. Senge
   Routledge Classics, London
   ISBN 10: 0-415-33641-4   ISBN 13: 978-0-415-33641-3

Diamond, Jared 1997
   Guns, Germs, and Steel — The Fates of Human Societies
   W.W.Norton Co., New York,

Diamond, Jared 2005
   Collapse – How Societies Choose to Fail or Succeed
   Viking, Penguin Group, New York

Durant, Will and Ariel 1968
   The Lessons Of History
   Simon and Schuster, New York

Hawkins, David R M.D., Ph.D. 1995
   Power vs. Force
   Hay House, Carlsbad, CA

Heider, John 1985
   The Tao of Leadership
   Bantam Books, New York

Jaworski, Joseph 2011
   Synchronicity, The Inner Path of Leadership
   Barrett-Koehler Publishers, Inc., San Francisco

Killion, Joellen P., Lynn A. Simmons 1992
   The Zen of Facilitation
   Journal of Staff Development, Summer 1992, Vol. 13, No.3,
   Oxford, OH

Mayer, Elizabeth Lloyd 2008
   Extraordinary Knowing
   Bantam Dell, New York   ISBN: 978-0-553-38223-5

Meadows, Donnela, Jørgen Randers, Dennis Meadows 1972, 2004
   Limits to Growth: The 30-Year Update.
   Chelsea Green Publishing Company and Earthscan.

Raphael, Daniel 1999
    Sacred Relationships, A Guide to Authentic Loving
    Origin Press   ISBN: 1-57983-001-3
    PO Box 151117, San Rafael, CA 94915
    www.OriginPress.org

Semler, Ricardo, 1993
    MAVERICK —
    The Success Story Behind the World's Most Unusual Workplace
    Warner Books, New York

Senge, Peter M. 1994
    The Fifth Discipline
    Currency Doubleday, New York

Wright, Kurt 1998
    Breaking the Rules
    ISBN: 0-9614383-3-9
    CPM Publishing, Boise, ID

❖

Is democracy as we know it the last improvement
possible in government?
Is it not possible to take a step further towards
the rights of man?
There will never be a free and enlightened State
until the State comes to recognize the individual
as a higher and independent power,
from which all its own power and authority is derived
and treats him accordingly."

    Henry David Thoreau, "Essay On Civil Disobedience," 1846

BIO:

Daniel Raphael is an independent thinker who is a Viet Nam veteran; with 18 years' experience working in adult felony criminal corrections; father of three and grandfather of two children; small business owner, inventor, and manufacturer of a household product; author and publisher of several books, manuscripts, and numerous articles; principal of Daniel Raphael, Ph.D. Consulting, since 2003. Daniel has taught numerous spirituality and social sustainability classes and workshops nationally and internationally and is well prepared to enlighten and entertain you.

Remarkably he has had a prescient sense of the future since his early childhood. These skills coupled with his deep meditation practices have enabled him to become an effective holistic life coach and spiritual counselor, and have given him insights into the lives of his clients; and, into macro perspectives of the world. These gifts have been useful to him to see the necessity of social sustainability.

You are invited to inform yourself about social sustainability via his "Dropbox" link of daily posts related to social sustainability:

https://www.dropbox.com/s/2cvd4gqmrwtsyza/POSTS%20%26%20DropBox%20LI NKS.docx?dl=0

Education
Bachelor of Science, (Sociology), Arizona State University, Tempe, Arizona.
Master of Science (Educationally and Culturally Disadvantaged), Western Oregon State University, Monmouth, Oregon.
Doctor of Philosophy (Spiritual Metaphysics), U. of Metaphysics, Sedona, Arizona.
Masters Dissertation: *A Loving-God Theology* ~ Doctoral Dissertation: *A Pre-Creation Theology*

Writer, Author, Publisher
(1992) *Developing A Loving-God Theology*
(1997) *Bedtime Stories from Angels to a Lonely Child*, (unpublished)
(1999) *Sacred Relationship, A Guide to Authentic Loving*
(2002) *What Was God Thinking?!*
(2015) *Social Sustainability Handbook for Community-Builders*

Contact Information:
Daniel Raphael, Ph.D.
Social Sustainability Leadership Training and Consulting
daniel.raphaelphd@gmail.com   Cell: 303.641.1115
PO Box 2408
Evergreen, CO 80437 USA

"...History demonstrates that it takes many
decades and centuries to build a civilization,
but only years or decades for it to
decline and even collapse.
Building a sustainable global
civilization will require conscious and
deliberate intention to initiate,
and may take decades and centuries
to complete — that and an awareness
that social change will be a
constant annoyance until then."